SO LET IT BE WRITTEN

**THE BIOGRAPHY OF
METALLICA'S JAMES HETFIELD**

By Mark Eglinton

LESSER
GODS

FIRST PUBLISHED IN THE UNITED STATES OF AMERICA IN 2017 BY:
Lesser Gods, 15 W. 36th St., 8th Fl., New York, NY 10018,
an imprint of Overamstel Publishers, Inc.
PHONE (646) 850-4201
www.lessergodsbooks.com

Originally published in the United Kingdom by
Independent Music Press in 2010

DISTRIBUTED BY: Consortium Book Sales & Distribution,
34 13th Ave. NE #101, Minneapolis, MN 55413
PHONE (800) 283-3572
www.cbsd.com

FIRST U.S. UPDATED EDITION APRIL 2017
PRINTED AND BOUND IN THE U.S.A.
ISBN: 978-1-944713-19-5
LIBRARY OF CONGRESS CONTROL NUMBER: 2017930070

TABLE OF CONTENTS

FOREWORD

I can't remember the exact year it was when we all first met, but I know it was way before Metallica came into their own and became the band that they are today. Having mutual friends, we used to go to a lot of New Year's parties and such. Seeing James perform for the first time I was truly taken aback. It was great watching this guy perform. I went to the party expecting to see James singing and playing guitar, but he was playing drums, which blew me away. He was even cooler now than before. James made a huge imprint on the Bay Area with his distinct sound and attitude. He used to perform with the band Spastic Children, whose lead singer was Fred Cotton. Back then it really was all about good times and fun. From day one, James was the guy who started the movement and carried it out to the finish. In my mind he is one of the best, if not *the* best, metal guitarist/lyricists, for sure.

Thinking back, I can remember the moment when I knew that Metallica had really hit it big. I was playing in a basketball league at my local gym—a gym that happened to serve beer, by the way. After the game was over they were going to debut the new Metallica video. They dropped down a 50-inch projection screen and we waited. The video started. This was the first time I experienced the Metallica video for "Enter Sandman." For the band that never did videos and didn't care about airplay, they sure made one hell of a video! Watching it I said to myself, *Holy Smokes.* I knew from then on that Metallica was going to be one of the biggest bands ever.

Another story about James and Metallica that I will never forget took place on a sunny Sunday during our normal tailgate party for the Oakland Raiders. Every Sunday we all used to get together and tailgate before the games. On this particular Sunday, a rumor was going around that Metallica was going to be playing in the parking lot prior to the game. When I heard this I immediately thought it was bullshit, but people seemed to be sure that it was going to happen. Sure enough, on the other side of the parking lot there was a flatbed truck that was sealed up on all sides. Something was going on. When I saw the cars parked by the truck and I saw Hetfield get out, the grin on his face said it all. The next thing we knew the Metallica guys were heading into the flatbed. Within minutes, the front opened up and there was Metallica playing live at the tailgate of a Raiders game. This experience was totally mind-blowing and it is something that I will never forget.

That's one of the coolest things about James and Metallica. No matter how massive they have gotten, they still do unique things, like playing a tailgate party or countless other special gigs for their fans. Hopefully this book will rekindle certain special memories about one of metal's most charismatic and important individuals.

CHUCK BILLY OF TESTAMENT

INTRODUCTION

"James Hetfield is an unsung virtuoso. His guitar and vocal sound, along with his song ideas, have enabled Metallica to go from being classified alongside Motörhead and Venom, to being aligned with Bruce Springsteen and U2."

Those are the words of Alex Skolnick—guitarist in the thrash metal band Testament and a member of the Trans Siberian Orchestra. Skolnick is a virtuoso himself and an astute commentator on the world of rock music. Hetfield and Metallica went from the underground to thrash metal's top tier in 1986, and had even greater impact later in their career.

However, if you'd asked me in 1986 whether I expected to write about the life and career of James Hetfield, the answer would have been no. When I met that distinctly guarded guy that year after a show at the Edinburgh Playhouse in Scotland, I never imagined he would become a rock icon alongside Bono and Springsteen.

A lot has changed in thirty years, and the result is this: the first definitive biography of James Hetfield, front man of Metallica, by far the biggest heavy rock band of the modern era.

September 12, 1986: Metallica along with New York thrashers Anthrax were playing on their Damage, Inc. Tour to open-mouthed metal audiences throughout Europe. This tour changed the fabric of heavy music, with far more emphasis placed on speed and downright aggression thereafter. By this time in their career, Metallica had acquired a knack for complex song structures, and this combination of intelligence and ferocity was a killer mix.

However, this was no normal tour. Hetfield had broken his left wrist in a skateboarding accident. The result was a plaster cast, which ruled out guitar-playing for much of the tour.

Fortunately, John Marshall—guitar technician for Kirk Hammett, Metallica's other guitarist—filled in on rhythm guitar duties from somewhere in the wings while the band raged onstage. Hetfield was limited to singing. Later in the tour, and despite his initial reluctance, Marshall joined the band onstage, which must have been a surreal experience given the frenzied atmosphere at these seminal shows.

Hetfield's now legendary ability as a rhythm guitarist of almost inhuman precision was the one thing we didn't witness that night. However, his barked vocals and intimidating stage presence left a lasting impression.

After the show, Hetfield and the late Cliff Burton, Metallica's bass player at the time, wandered into a bar down the street from the venue, where a few of us were drinking and discussing the gig. Through a haze of time and alcohol, I vaguely recall a brief chat ensuing between the two of them. Burton was the more forthcoming of the two. Hetfield was somewhat distant. That didn't matter, though, as meeting members of the band after such a life-changing show was a huge bonus.

Our paths had crossed, though to them, it must have been just another forgettable encounter with fans.

The raw, evolving Metallica of 1986 were a very different band from the monster they would become. Their commercial zenith was still five years away. Similarly, the band members have grown over time, impacted by their huge commercial success and its accompanying public scrutiny. From day one, though, the driving force behind Metallica has been the axis of Hetfield and drummer Lars Ulrich. Their personal relationship has often been strained, which isn't surprising given their wildly different backgrounds. However, for the majority of Metallica's career, particularly prior to 1992, no one could question the aural results, and Hetfield's role was significant.

James Hetfield is a guitarist of otherworldly ability, a front man of gargantuan stature and a much-underrated lyricist and songwriter. But he is more than just a great and influential musician. Hetfield is a more sensitive and thoughtful person than his public persona has suggested. Many are familiar with the hirsute, hard-drinking man of hunting and hot-rods, but that's not all he is. This book tries to understand, demystify and humanize a rock legend who, for most of his career, has remained impenetrable.

CHAPTER 1
JAMIE

People debate whether human beings' traits are determined by genetics or by our upbringing and environment. While elements of both are true, stress and family upheaval in childhood have significant effects.

As far as environments go, Downey, California, is as neutral and unremarkable as many of the other towns in the area. With a history that dates back to the Spanish colonial times of the early 1770s, the city is located at the confluence of several major highways. It's approximately thirteen miles southeast of the bright lights and perceived opportunity of Downtown Los Angeles.

The oldest surviving McDonald's is located on Downey's Lakewood Boulevard and has been there since 1953. It says a lot about the city's heritage that a fast food restaurant is one of its few landmarks. In addition, Taco Bell opened their first-ever restaurant in Downey in 1962.

James Alan Hetfield was born on August 3, 1963. In terms of music, this was a momentous year for Downey, not just because a future rock icon was born. That same year, singing siblings The Carpenters, who were still teenagers, moved to Downey from their native Connecticut.

James Hetfield's mother, Cynthia—a light-opera singer—had been married prior to meeting James's father, Virgil. Cynthia was, as James once described her, "a Berkeley Mom," and was apparently open to loud music and long hair. Virgil was a truck driver, with a small distribution operation of his own. Cynthia undertook the bulk of the childcare in the early days, as Virgil would often be away from home on extended business trips. Although widely regarded as a kind man, he was—in contrast to his laid-back wife—considerably more reserved and conservative.

James had two half-brothers, Chris and Dave, who were eleven and twelve years older, as well as an older sister, Deandra. They grew up in a loving environment that encouraged creativity.

One feature that bound the Hetfields together was The Church of Christian Science. In Christian Science, the focus of worship and belief is God. Founded in 1866 by Mary Baker Eddy—who had endured chronic childhood illness—the belief system maintains that the power of healing is available to all of us and that we need to refer to Biblical scriptures for the answers. The church considers the universe and humanity to be of a spiritual nature, as opposed to being material entities. The suggestion is that, due to the "absolute purity" and perfection of God, He could not have created sin, disease and death—and therefore they do not exist.

James reflected on his religious upbringing in an interview with *Playboy* in 2001: "I was raised a Christian Scientist, which is a strange religion. The main rule is: God will fix everything—your body is just a shell, you don't need doctors. It was alienating and hard to understand." This restrictive approach to medicine would have a dramatic impact on the Hetfield family and on James himself during his adolescence.

James was close to his half-brothers. David in particular was a big influence. Chris had left the home already. Even at a very early age, James was steered in a musical direction, mainly by his mother, who encouraged him down that familiar route of piano lessons. Hetfield started at the age of nine and continued for almost two years. He showed a lot of promise, but by his own admission, it wasn't fulfilling playing classical tunes. That wasn't the music that kids in California were hearing on the radio.

It wasn't wasted time, though. In recent years, James has acknowledged the importance of his early exposure to a two-handed instrument, even if the results weren't exactly what he was looking for. He admitted that the cookies that were offered, presumably as an incentive at the end of each session, were a big draw as well.

Before long, Hetfield's young head was being turned by David's drum kit—and the louder and rockier options it offered. David regularly played drums in a band called The Bitter End. Armed with a new and burning desire to play guitar, it was a matter of *when*—not *if*—his younger sibling would ultimately head in the same direction.

A lot of James's favorite bands were the heavier acts of the time, like Black Sabbath, ZZ Top and KISS. However, if there was one band that fueled his desire to rock out, it was Aerosmith.

Aerosmith were a blues-influenced, swaggering rock band with a heavy sound derived from the likes of the Rolling Stones. They liked to party and were a pretty debauched outfit during the 1970s. Despite living on the edge somewhat, they propped themselves up on stage long enough to do live shows in the Downey area. James attended his first Aerosmith concert at the LA Forum in 1978.

In Joe Perry, Aerosmith had a cool guitarist that caught James's eye and he could see himself mirroring that image.

James was fortunate that David was in college—training to be a public accountant—which meant that he was often away studying. His considerable record collection—which included not only hard rock bands but also a load of old rock 'n' roll 45s—was at the mercy of young James. He took full advantage by making his brother's vinyl collection his bedrock of influence.

It didn't go unnoticed by David, and as part of the documentary *Some Kind of Monster*, James sheepishly admitted: "I'd always leave the turntable on and he'd know. I'd come home and get busted because the turntable was still on." David always seemed to know what his younger brother was up to, as James admitted when describing getting caught: "'Jamie, were you playing my records?' He called me Jamie when I was a kid."

Another guy in the Downey scene was Ron McGovney, who played a major and often undervalued role in the band we now know as Metallica. McGovney felt that he and James were kindred spirits. Ron recalled how they got together: "We met at East Middle School in Downey at the age of about eleven. We both went to different elementary schools, so we didn't know each other before then. I really lived in Norwalk, the next city over, but my parents got me into Downey schools, which they thought were better."

In McGovney, James had a likeminded friend. Their musical tastes weren't aligned, although that gradually changed. McGovney explained: "Neither of us was in any social or sports group. We were the outcasts, you might say. He used to make fun of my Elvis sticker I had on my folder, and I made fun of the Aerosmith sticker he had on his." McGovney added, "He is the one who really got me into listening to hard rock and metal. Before that, I listened to stuff like the Doobie Brothers, Fleetwood Mac and, of course, Elvis Presley."

It's worth noting McGovney's mention of sports. Due to his family's religious beliefs, James shied away from participating in physically active sports for fear of getting hurt. Children often relish the bonding experience found in team sports. Its absence likely contributed to James's quiet demeanor, and he relied on his growing interest in music instead.

James was beginning to ask questions about his family's religious beliefs. As part of the *Playboy* interview in 2001, he suggested that he found it difficult to understand the health implications of his religious upbringing: "My dad taught Sunday school—he was into it. It was pretty much forced upon me. We had these little testimonials, and there was a girl that had her arm broken. She stood up and said, "I broke my arm but now, look, it's all better." But it was just, like, mangled. Now that I think about it, it was pretty disturbing."

Unfortunately, a life-changing roadblock was looming large. His parents' divorce in 1976 shook the family unit to the core.

Hetfield explained to *Playboy*: "Dad went on a "business trip" . . . for more than a few years, you know? I was beginning junior high. It was hidden that he was gone. Finally, my Mom said, 'Dad is not coming back.' And that was pretty difficult."

Daily life was tense in the household at times. While Cynthia worked hard to balance home and a career—with inevitable pressure to be at home—James and his sister argued frequently. This escalated to one occasion when James burned his sister with hot oil, which he later admitted was a step too far.

The absence of a father figure at home did not help. What wasn't yet apparent was that Cynthia was suffering from cancer. Given her religious beliefs, this was not going to be an easy battle. As if there weren't enough challenges for the family, money, or the lack of it, became a pressing issue. James had to bring in some income for the household, and he got a job.

As an aspiring rock star in his own mind, regular work wasn't something he was particularly keen on. To make matters worse, his mother insisted that nobody would hire him unless he cut his hair. This, according to James, wasn't happening anytime soon. "Well, long hair's part of music, Mom. Y'know, if I've got short hair I can't rock, you know. There's no way," Hetfield later admitted.

Long hair intact, James saw music as his chosen escape. James actively sought to join—or, ideally, form—a band. In addition to McGovney, a fellow student named Dave Marrs had similar taste in late 1970s rock. It was inevitable that they gravitated toward each other.

"Ron and I were actually friends first, and we all knew James but he was never into our little clique of friends that we had," Marrs told the author. "Then in tenth grade I had him in a biology class and I had my KISS T-shirt on and he had his Aerosmith shirt on and we just became really good friends. Everything kind of clicked from there."

Hetfield, McGovney, and Marrs ran in the same circles—largely based on their love of music—and this bond lasted for several years. The group spent time doing the kinds of things kids do, including hanging around the local miniature golf course, where there were video games, and a bowling alley, where the trio played pool. It was nothing out of the ordinary. It was regular teenage life in suburban California.

Rock music was high in the pecking order for these likeminded teenagers. While James spent most of his time thinking about how to join a band, he wasn't without talent in other departments. "I would say he was a pretty [normal] student generally," McGovney recalled. "Practicing guitar took up a lot of his time! Even then it was obvious that music was the way forward. But he did excel at art classes, though, and could probably have made a career out of that."

That early artistic talent proved useful in future years. Hetfield's ability to create an image—whether visually for an album cover or lyrically for a song—had intrinsic value in his future bands, most notably Metallica.

As much as James wanted to form a band—and as desperately as he aspired to be the driving force behind it—the outfit that offered James his first chance to rock, called Obsession, was the brainchild of a couple of brothers named Ron and Rich Veloz.

Marrs recalled: "I was real good friends with the Veloz brothers and they had something going on with their band. They had another friend with them called Jim Arnold as well. They said, 'We need another guitar player,' and that's how James ended up joining Obsession."

Arnold told the author about the first time he went round to James's house: "The thing I remember most is that he had a life-sized silhouette on his bedroom wall. From what I remember, it was Steve Tyler and Joe Perry of Aerosmith, and I think he said his mother had painted it for him. It was very cool!"

Obsession consisted of Hetfield on guitar, Ron Veloz on bass, Rich Veloz on drums and Jim Arnold on lead guitar. Every band needs a kick-ass road crew, so McGovney and Marrs were drafted. Marrs admitted that their role was overstated: "We were more like friends than actually roadies, really."

The Veloz boys' garage became the venue for rehearsals, with Marrs and McGovney staffing a crude control panel to give the place some basic lighting effects. Marrs recalled: "They just played, like, backyard parties back then. They were just, like, your average garage band. They did UFO covers, and I think they did 'Communication Breakdown,' good songs like that. I remember that the Veloz brothers [had] some traffic lights or something, and they hooked them up into the garage and we'd go up there and play with the lights. We were fifteen-year-old kids and we didn't know what we were actually doing up there, we definitely didn't. It was a good time back then, though."

Arnold lived down the street at the time, and he, too, has fond memories of Obsession's early garage days: "We built a wall inside that garage and soundproofed one half of it using old cardboard and carpet. James only lived a few miles from there, and he would use his mom's car to drive over, or we would go and pick him up. We spent a lot of time in that garage; it was our party and practice place."

Although no recordings of the band exist, it is safe to say that the Hetfield of Obsession and the one we know now were poles apart. His voice at the time had little of the full-bore bellow that he would develop in the late 1980s and none of the harmony that would bleed into Metallica's work in the 1990s. His guitar-playing—an act of un-stoppable brutality in later years—was reputedly just passable in those formative days. He was, after all, still a teenager.

As an adolescent, James's musical tastes were pretty diverse. Like most teenagers discovering the buzz of concerts, the group of friends would take in any gig they could, relying on rides from their patient parents to venues in the wider LA area.

Marrs recalled one in particular: "I actually remember going to a Blondie concert with James back then. It was in the Greek Theatre, which is in LA, and I can remember his mom taking us there and then my mom came to pick us up. It was just weird to see Blondie and stuff with James and now you have to consider that they're both in the Rock & Roll Hall of Fame."

Obsession's days were numbered from the start. There wasn't much variety in the generic covers that the band played. The fact that they couldn't decide who would sing didn't help either. James traded vocal duties with Arnold and Ron Veloz.

After about eighteen months, Hetfield and Arnold left Obsession to form a new project with Jim's brother Chris, named Syrinx. That band played covers of songs by the influential prog rock three-piece Rush.

The origin of the name was obvious: "Temple of Syrinx" from Rush's seminal concept record, *2112*. This band was short-lived. Luckily, there was a more durable band around the corner, which had a big impact on James's career. "James was very cool and fun to be around," Arnold con-firmed, "but more importantly, he introduced us to a lot of cool music that was not mainstream at the time: Scorpions, Rush, Iron Maiden and bands like that. Back then we had never heard of such bands."

Lurking in the background was a far bigger issue. For a long while, James's mother, Cynthia, had hidden her failing health from her children. Before too long, she needed hospital attention, but she declined conventional medical treatment.

Cynthia passed away in 1979. James was in the eleventh grade, and he moved to nearby Brea to live with his half-brother David, who had recently gotten married. Although James rarely discussed the constraints of his religious upbringing, such upheaval must have taken an emotional toll. He felt that he lacked control over his personal circumstances, and this became a key part of his life, manifesting itself in numerous forms.

Marrs recalled that Cynthia's passing came as a complete shock: "We were outside between classes and James said, 'Well, I'm going to have to move to Brea,' and we said, 'Why are you going to do that?' and James told us, 'My mom just passed away.' We never knew she was sick, we never knew anything. You have to remember, I was always with him and his mother—spending nights at his house and stuff like that—so it was pretty hard. He moved to live with his [half-brother]. I kept in real good contact with him, though, even though he was living further away. As a matter of fact we used to go over there quite a bit."

Arnold also kept in touch with James: "We would talk on the phone, and he'd stay at my parents' house at the weekends. I knew he was breaking off to form a new band and writing music."

While Arnold continued to be a friend, he wasn't convinced that James's musical career was going anywhere: "He would tell me of songs he was writing and that he was going to form a 'heavy metal' band.

Back then, heavy metal was not very popular. At the time I didn't think he would go anywhere with it, but boy was I wrong!"

Living in Brea—fifteen miles east of Downey—meant that James attended Brea Olinda High School. Brea is another quiet suburban town, with a population of only 35,000. It was a change of pace from the much bigger and grittier Downey.

After losing his mother, moving in with David and going to a new school, James was going through a difficult period. In terms of his musical aspirations, though, moving to Brea worked out well. Before long, a kid named Jim Mulligan appeared on the scene, and he was a drummer on a mission.

Hetfield and Mulligan had a lot in common, including a shared passion for music—although Mulligan's tastes were considerably more academic. Regardless of any stylistic disagreement, they were soon playing songs during their lunch breaks, creating the kind of noise that sent other kids into hiding. All except for a guy named Hugh Tanner, who totally "got" what they were all about.

At that time, punk rock was the flavor of the day at Brea Olinda High School. Long hair was not. Tanner was a junior and Hetfield was a senior, but the two had some things in common. They were both starting at a new school, they both had long hair and they were in the same English class.

Interestingly, Tanner has never publicly discussed his relationship with Hetfield—or his involvement with the band that would become Metallica—until now. He explained, "My involvement with James Hetfield and Lars Ulrich and Metallica has been something speculated on for some time but is something I have shared only with close family.

It was not until the Internet brought forth 1980s interviews from Ron McGovney and [Metallica's first guitarist] Dave Mustaine that a few people began to ask me if I was *that* Hugh Tanner. To some I would say yes, and to others I would say no."

Tanner said "yes" for the first time in thirty years and agreed to be interviewed for this book. He easily remembered the stories and the associated events: "The [local people] I was jamming with liked my playing but did not like that I showed up to this jam session with an ugly Gibson ES335! It was much like Ted Nugent's Birdland guitar but had a cutaway at the top. For whatever reason I could wail on that guitar, but it looked like I was a set musician for Billy Ray Cyrus. Fortunately, I did have a knock-off Flying V at home. I was not keen on it because it was maroon. I took the pieces to the school wood-shop to sand it down and refinish it. James ended up helping me to refinish the guitar in gloss white, which we did in my garage. We got overspray all over my dad's new Mercedes, though."

Hetfield and Tanner quickly bonded and became lasting friends. Tanner was aware of James's difficult family circumstances, and he recognized the potential problems: "Starting a new school is pretty intimidating to begin with, but when you don't really fit in . . . things can be tough."

Despite James's bereavement and upheaval, he dealt with his situation extremely well. Tanner recalled: "Interestingly, James was grounded, likeable, funny and very polite to my parents. He did not talk much about his family loss and all I really knew was that he was living with his [half-brother] and [his] wife."

Tanner's mother recognized that things were hard for James, and she even brought up the possibility of James and his sister coming to live with them. She felt that it might take some pressure off David, who was still settling into his married life. That thoughtful suggestion was never made to James, though, and things remained as they were.

In their classes, Hetfield and Tanner focused more on drawing pictures of stage-sets and writing song titles than on the lessons being taught. Tanner remembered that English classes were particularly "productive."

"We spent time drawing pictures of Iron Maiden's 'Eddie' as well as thinking about lyrics and songs," Tanner recalled. What might have seemed insignificant back then was that, amid such humble and innocent surroundings, Hetfield was creating the foundations of some songs that appeared on Metallica's debut album, *Kill 'Em All.* Hetfield conceived seminal songs like "Metal Militia," "Seek and Destroy" and "Motorbreath," while Tanner provided enthusiastic support.

American bands were no longer hitting the spot for Hetfield and Tanner. Aerosmith were not heavy enough, and KISS were "bubble-gum," in Tanner's words. Their heads turned towards faster bands coming out of the UK like Judas Priest, Motörhead and Iron Maiden. Tanner recalled: "Van Halen's 'life is a party' attitude was fun, but it did not completely satisfy the pent-up adrenaline of a high school boy who didn't know why but just wanted to break *something*."

Outside of school hours, James often went over to Tanner's house to practice. Tanner vividly recalled, "James would come over and we would spend time trading riffs, playing solos and experimenting with turning riffs into actual songs." When teaming up with Marrs and McGovney, James and Tanner dipped their toes into the flamboyant 1980s LA music scene, which was populated by myriad glam/hair metal bands. Ratt, Snow and Du Brow (who later became Quiet Riot) were the better known acts. There were regular shows at the legend-ary Whisky on Sunset Strip and The Troubadour on Santa Monica Boulevard.

It was an exciting time in LA, with legendary acts like Mötley Crüe waiting in the wings. Tanner recalled, "We all used to go up to LA to see the up-and-comers on the club circuit. The four of us had a blast!"

It was an important time in and out of the classroom, and the school was the lyrical inspiration of some seminal early Metallica songs. Tanner's bedroom was likewise important, as he confirmed: "My old room was the birthplace of riff inspirations for these songs. Not just that, there were others which may have been lost or got morphed into other ideas."

This key period was significant for the direction of Hetfield and his future bands. The quality of the recorded material was, by Tanner's own admission, "very, very poor." It was mostly documented on an old Teac reel-to-reel his father had brought back from his time as a spy-pilot in Vietnam. Nevertheless, it documented the band's musical output and represented a fascinating ground-zero for some of the most important tracks in metal history.

Tanner remembered Hetfield having a great sense of humor: "I was experimenting with my first whammy bar and one time it made a noise like a walrus farting. James came to a dead stop and said, 'What the hell was that?' We laughed hysterically." James had a lot of qualities that made his stoic determination to be a rock star much more likely. Tanner summed him up best: "Guard down . . . funny . . . laid-back but serious . . . cool but never lazy . . . focused but not overly intense."

Despite all these worthy attributes, Hetfield was not particularly scholarly or technical in a musical sense. This is surprising given the amazingly disciplined technician he became. Tanner did recognize a rare quality in his friend, though, and James soon put it into practice with remarkable effect. "What I viewed as his greatest gift," suggested Tanner, "was tying riffs together into a sensible kick-ass song."

An informal jamming group soon became the first band assembled by Hetfield. The group was called Phantom Lord—which Metallica fans will recognize as the title of a song on *Kill 'Em All.* Phantom Lord was short-lived, with Mulligan on drums, Tanner on guitar and Hetfield on guitar and vocals. Marrs recalled what Phantom Lord were about: "They would do just covers of different things like Iron Maiden, etc. They had a song called 'Handsome Ransom' back then and a riff similar to the one from 'No Remorse' came out of that. Mulligan was a really good drummer, mind you."

Mulligan might have been too cerebral for a full-bore rock band. He wasn't into the aggressive, heavy nature of Tanner and Hetfield's material, and both Tanner and Hetfield noticed. "Jim was a great guy, solid drummer and did not rock the boat, but I did not sense the right chemistry," Tanner said. "Jim and I had jammed with Scott Bell from the band Joker, and we nailed side one of Rush's *2112,* but Jim was just too intellectual for metal. It didn't fit and James knew it too."

There wasn't a set bassist, although several players went in and out. This embryonic outfit only lasted a few months, until James graduated from high school and moved back to Downey. Upon moving, Hetfield sent Tanner a note saying that while he wasn't thrilled with some aspects of school life, he had enjoyed playing music together. Hetfield suggested that one day they might be in a stadium-crushing rock band.

In the portion of the yearbook where seniors provide their memories of school and plans for the future, Hetfield wrote:

Likes: *heavy metal rock, water skiing, going to concerts.*

Dislikes: *disco, punk.*

Quotes: "*Long Live Rock.*"

Plans: *Play music get rich.*

The move back to Downey coincided with some good fortune. McGovney's parents had three properties in the area that were earmarked by the government to be torn down in order to make way for the 105 Freeway. They let their son and James live in one of them rent-free until it was demolished. There was a garage space that was begging to be turned into a rehearsal studio.

While neither was skilled in DIY handiwork, they turned the garage into a custom-made band area. McGovney recalled, "We fixed the garage up into a kind of studio and James and I insulated, painted it and put down a red carpet!"

It's unclear when Phantom Lord ceased to be. The edges of Phantom Lord and the next band, Leather Charm, are blurred. McGovney said: "I am quite confused about how things went down. I remember Phantom Lord was really just Hugh and James. Then Leather Charm got together. However, I have my high school yearbook signed by James saying that he 'hopes the Charm will happen.' So maybe Phantom Lord was actually still when we were in high school."

Regardless of the exact timing, Phantom Lord soon morphed into the more glam-sounding Leather Charm. This was the last stop for the train that led to Metallica and was a stop where people disembarked.

The living arrangement allowed James to focus on music in a custom-made space. He didn't have to worry about getting a "real" job and paying rent, which was quite a luxury for a teenager.

James's father visited the house occasionally, as McGovney recalled: "I met his father, Virgil, when he came over to my house that James shared with me. He was very nice to me. He actually knew my parents through the trucking business that they were all involved with."

Despite still being a rudimentary cover band, Leather Charm was a significant step forward from Phantom Lord, and certainly from Obsession. Leather Charm began working on a few original tunes. Hetfield wrote songs that contained elements of what would become "Hit the Lights," which appeared on *Kill 'Em All.*

Wanting to be seen as a more commanding front man, Hetfield seemed to take control of his musical destiny. He also encouraged McGovney to come along for the ride, helping him to learn bass.

The noise that came out of that insulated garage did not sound like a polished rock band. McGovney was improving at the bass under Hetfield's instruction, but he described the music as "some really terrible stuff."

Tanner recalled that his parents would only let him continue with the band if his grades at school were okay. "They weren't!" he admitted.

Tanner backed out of a career playing music, which allowed James to take on full leadership. Although Tanner didn't completely disappear from Hetfield's life, his musical involvement with him ended here. "I still cannot explain the tug I had calling me to step aside, versus throwing up a thunderous middle finger and pushing forward," Tanner said. "But the ship sailed and I chose to stay on land."

Meanwhile, across the city in Newport Beach, a gawky Danish kid with a taste for the so-called "New Wave of British Heavy Metal" (NWOBHM) was planning his own future. The crossing of paths that followed would dramatically impact the lives and careers of both him and James Hetfield.

CHAPTER 2
ENTER LARS

The formative years of James Hetfield and Lars Ulrich were worlds apart both geographically and in terms of privilege. Ulrich's liberal upbringing is well documented elsewhere, but it's important to have a broad understanding of it in order to grasp why Hetfield and Ulrich worked so effectively together.

Lars Ulrich was also born in the summer of 1963 in an affluent northern suburb of Copenhagen, Denmark, called Gentofte. His father, Torben, was an internationally renowned tennis player, as well an accomplished jazz musician, who traveled the world for his career. While at home, he immersed himself in philosophy and filmmaking.

On a musical level, the Ulrich family was rather well connected too. Prior to Lars's birth, Torben would frequently travel to London to perform with jazz greats like Humphrey Lyttleton. Lars's childhood involved exposure to music that few could hope to enjoy. He became obsessed with rock music, with Deep Purple being an early favorite.

At fourteen years old, Lars had a drum kit. He would hammer out Deep Purple and KISS songs in his bedroom, while his musically open-minded parents took their son's passion for heavy rock in stride. Ulrich's privileged upbringing, in contrast to Hetfield's grittier, working-class childhood was critical to their relationship and resulted in a powerful chemistry.

In August 1980, with Torben's tennis career easing into a veteran phase, the family emigrated to the wealthy LA suburb of Newport Beach. A good friend of Torben's, Australian tennis star Roy Emerson, lived there.

Lars had potential as a tennis player, so the United States represented the best training opportunity and a more favorable climate. His parents also recognized their son's love for music, so they felt that a move abroad would allow Lars's definitive passion to surface.

While Lars enjoyed tennis, music—specifically heavy music from Europe—was steadily winning his heart and mind. Always inquisitive and attending Corona del Mar High School, he soon got the UK magazine *Sounds*, which served as his direct line to Europe and the emerging NWOBHM. It was the Emerson family that received the imported magazine, and Lars would go over and pick it up with increasing enthusiasm.

Very few people were tuned into this new British movement. These were the days long before the Internet, file-sharing or any other means of hearing new bands besides reading about them and sending away for imported singles or tapes. Lars was several steps ahead of the pack.

One guy who knew all about the NWOBHM scene was John Kornarens. Three years older than Lars and James, Kornarens grew up in Southern California and moved around a lot when he was young. In the early 1970s, he found that he was attracted to heavy music. "As an eight-year-old I was into heavy music," he told the author. "I sent away for my first *K-Tel* record and it had 'You Really Got Me' by The Kinks on it, and I just kept coming back to that song." Kornarens found himself drawn to Black Sabbath and Led Zeppelin. As a result of his interest in World War II, he got into Blue Öyster Cult because he liked the military symbol on their *Secret Treaties* album. "I was the only kid in junior high with a BÖC T-shirt and I think everyone thought I was some kind of satanic weirdo!"

By the time 1980 rolled around, Kornarens was a huge devotee of heavy rock music. A year earlier, he had found *Sounds* magazine and was attracted to music that nobody else was listening to. "I always tried to be the first guy out of the gate as far as what was new and was always looking for stuff that was off the radar," Kornarens continued. "Through *Sounds* I got into the imported material and sometime in 1980 I got the Angel Witch single."

Angel Witch, while never enjoying the success that bands like Saxon and Iron Maiden achieved, were one of the important early exponents of the NWOBHM. Having an imported Angel Witch single was something of a coup.

Given the huge population of Southern California, it was unlikely that the few people following a new and distant music scene would come together, particularly since Ulrich lived sixty miles down the coast. However, they did find one another, and Kornarens vividly remembers where: "I went to see the Michael Schenker Group at The Country Club, and afterward in the parking lot I looked and saw a little guy with long hair wearing a Saxon tour shirt. I thought I was the only person in the country who knew who Saxon were!"

The two teenagers were drawn to each other immediately. Kornarens recalled, "I walked right up to him and we started talking about Saxon. Then I told him I had the new Angel Witch single and he did a back-flip." The two talked for a while about all the bands they liked. "We made an instant connection," said Kornarens.

What happened next was a good example of what makes Lars Ulrich unique. Instead of reconnecting after a few days or weeks, Ulrich appeared at Kornarens's front door the very next morning—eager to rifle through his record collection. His enthusiasm and passion took the rather laid-back Kornarens by surprise: "He used to drive his mother's car—an old brown AMC Pacer—which was probably the ugliest car ever designed. He came up the next day and we spent hours talking and listening to music."

They quickly became good friends, as Kornarens confirmed: "I think I was down at his place a few days later and we kind of became the NWOBHM Beavis and Butthead!" Ulrich and Kornarens would scour record shops for new material. "We'd drive up to places like Moby Disc and see what new stuff they had," Kornarens recalled.

Prior to meeting Ulrich, Kornarens had picked up a fanzine entitled *The New Heavy Metal Review*, which was founded by a tape-trader named Brian Slagel from Woodland Hills, an area west of LA.

At the time, buying traded tapes was one of the only ways to hear about new bands, and a network of tape-traders sprang up. Their primary business was mailing tapes of bands and demos to likeminded fans, some of whom were overseas. It was the akin to Internet file-sharing, except the quality was typically poor, given that the recordings were often thirdhand or worse.

Regardless of the rough quality, traded tapes were a big part of the music scene, and Slagel was one of the first in the LA area to get seriously involved. "He was just into trading stuff, and when I first got a hold of him I went out to his house to collect some heavy stuff I'd ordered," Kornarens recalled.

As Ulrich and Kornarens saw more of each other, Slagel was gradually absorbed into the group. That connection was of vital importance to the destiny of Ulrich and Hetfield. Kornarens, Ulrich and Slagel would tour the area looking for new material that nobody had. "We'd go record shopping in my old Volkswagen Scirocco, and I was always the point guy," Kornarens recalled.

Given that most of these record shops were scattered around faraway places like Long Beach and Torrance, Kornarens usually had to drive and pick up the other two. "Brian would be in the front and Lars would be in the back and when we arrived at each record store, Lars would somehow manage to climb over Brian to get out, even when the car hadn't come to a complete stop!"

Ulrich was always keen to get the first look at the record bins. "By the time we got there, Lars had probably been through three racks and found the only copy of this band or that band!" Kornarens said. In addition to patrolling record stores with Slagel like some kind of unstoppable record-buying delta-force, Kornarens and Ulrich ordered new material from ads they saw in *Sounds* magazine, and Lars would stop at nothing to get what he wanted. "We'd ordered the new

Holocaust record or something and Lars called one day to say the package had arrived," Kornarens said.

What Kornarens did not know before his hour-long drive was that there was, as Lars put it, "a problem with John's Holocaust record." Ulrich had opened the package and put one of the records on the stove—where it got badly warped—and this was Kornarens's copy. "And the next day I even tried to get my mother to iron the fucking thing out!" Kornarens recalled.

As 1980 moved into 1981, the distance between Ulrich and Hetfield was shrinking, given the tight-knit nature of the LA metal scene. Unbeknownst to them, they had a common link in the form of Hugh Tanner. "I came across Lars when James and I were still jamming together because I answered an ad in the *Recycler* magazine where Lars listed himself as a 'drummer from Europe.'" Tanner recalled. Ulrich's ad mentioned a raft of NWOBHM bands.

"So I called and we jammed," Tanner confirmed. Also at that first session was guitarist Jeff "Woop" Warner, who, according to Tanner, had a good rock 'n' roll look and sound. Warner later joined the hair metal band Black 'N Blue. That first session made Tanner think that Hetfield's need to be a front man would easily be fulfilled.

Tanner and Ulrich continued to jam together. The first time that Hetfield went along to Newport Beach was the first time he and Ulrich were in the same room together. James was, as Tanner remembered, "thoroughly unimpressed" with Lars's drumming ability at the time, but Ulrich was nothing if not determined. Tanner said, "It did not seem to bother him or faze him that although he was nearly eighteen and just learning the drums, he could not be a rock star in a short order of time. He proclaimed things with such confidence . . . he sought opportunities [without] even thinking about rejection."

Ulrich only had a small drum kit back then, which Kornarens confirmed after an early visit to Ulrich's house: "There was this cupboard in between Lars's and his parents' rooms. He opens it up and there's a fucking drum kit in there. The problem was, there was hardly any room for him!"

Tanner remembered what his and Hetfield's initial impressions of Lars were following that first session: "James and I decided Lars was not ready." Hetfield was less complimentary when he told *Playboy* what he thought about his friend's drumming: "Lars had a pretty crappy drum kit, with one cymbal. It kept falling over, and we'd have to stop, and he'd pick the fucking thing up. He really was not a good drummer."

Tanner believed there were other issues: "Lars did not seem to fit personality-wise at that time. With James and me, we always seemed to think along the same lines." He didn't see Ulrich's self-confidence as a positive, and admitted, "Lars was out of my personal comfort zone."

However, Lars Ulrich's implacable belief in where he was going would soon be viewed as a positive, even by Tanner. Ulrich continued with his agenda, which included an ambitious solo trip to London to hang out with bands like NWOBHM pioneers Diamond Head.

Diamond Head were a heavy metal band formed in Stourbridge, England, in 1976. As one of the pioneers of the NWOBHM, they were an object of considerable adulation for Ulrich. Although they never fulfilled their early promise, they command almost mythical respect to this day, largely due to their connection to Metallica.

Kornarens recalled an amusing 'Lars moment': "So he phones me up after he'd been away for two weeks in London and tells me he's hanging out with Diamond Head. I say 'No way!' and the next thing he does is put [Diamond Head's singer] Sean Harris on the line." That summed up Lars's determination, and this unique ability to walk into any situation with supreme confidence would count for a lot in the months to come.

Slagel was feeding his increasing appetite for heavy metal with a job working at Oz Records, which gave him full access to a myriad of imported metal. He was contributing to *Sounds* magazine. In addition, after running into renowned *Kerrang!* writer Sylvie Simmons, he scored some column inches with Britain's most popular heavy rock magazine of that era.

Slagel felt that more people in LA's vibrant music scene should be aware of the NWOBHM, and decided he'd be the one to carry the baton. That meant setting up his own independent record label: Metal Blade Records.

Slagel scratched together money from his own resources and friends (Kornarens contributed). His goal was to release a compilation album featuring the best-sounding metal around. Like most entrepreneurs, Slagel openly admitted to "making every mistake humanly possible" in the early days. His job was made a lot easier by a lawyer friend who worked above Oz Records, who helped him navigate through the legal minefield of band contracts, royalties and licensing agreements.

Metal Blade's debut release was a compilation titled *The New Heavy Metal Review Presents Metal Massacre*, showcasing several of the area's hottest bands. Ulrich was enthused, so much so that he asked Slagel if he could submit a song for the record. Given that he didn't have a band, this was an audacious request, but it was not out of character. Unable to resist Ulrich's enthusiasm, Slagel agreed.

When he heard about Slagel's idea, Ulrich got in touch with Hetfield, whom he had not seen since their first meeting. He didn't call Hetfield directly, instead using Tanner as a buffer between them. Tanner recalled: "I hadn't heard much from Lars for six months or so. I got a call at home and recognized that accented voice with a ton of energy on the end of the line. But I was a little reluctant to put him in touch with James because I was aware of James's thoughts on his drumming."

Whatever he thought of Ulrich's drumming, Hetfield was interested in the idea, so he invited Lars over to the McGovney house to jam.

Hetfield and Ulrich saw each other a lot thereafter. The NWOBHM influences rubbed off on and ultimately replaced Hetfield's more traditional tastes. This was hardly surprising given Ulrich's all-consuming passion for that scene and the connections he'd carved out within it. (Lars had befriended Motörhead too.)

Kornarens was still seeing a lot of Lars and vividly remembered when James first appeared on his radar. "One day there's a knock on the door and here's Lars with this kid covered in acne," said Kornarens. "He was quiet and just kind of staring at me—I guess Lars had talked me up. He's got acne and a jeans jacket on with patches of bands like Aerosmith and maybe Ted Nugent."

Hetfield talked about the band posters on Kornarens's bedroom wall and acknowledged that they'd both been at the same Aerosmith concert in 1978. Hetfield warmed to Kornarens's friendly approach, but from that day forward, Hetfield would see far more of Ulrich than Kornarens.

Like many teenagers, James had discovered alcohol. Kornarens re-called a later visit: "We're sitting on the blue sofa in my parents' sitting room being offered my sister's chocolate chip cookies, and James pulls out some whisky and starts drinking it." Despite being told to stop, Hetfield laughed and continued drinking from his flask.

Kornarens didn't take long to figure out what Hetfield was all about. He explained, "I knew his outlet was music. He was not a happy person and he used to drink. And also he didn't really have a job. He had a creative side and he was nice, but he definitely had a dark side about him. He just wasn't . . . perky."

As Hetfield told *Playboy*, "My mother had just passed away. Everyone was the enemy back then. I wasn't the best at talking."

The Hetfield and Ulrich connection was beginning to cementing and, with the possibility of forming a band and producing music for an exciting compilation, events began to move quickly.

CHAPTER 3

"METTALLICA"

By 1982, Hetfield, Ulrich and McGovney were spending a lot of time practicing in McGovney's house. Occasionally, Lars stayed there rather than undertake the long trek back to Newport Beach. Hetfield, Ulrich and McGovney were all behind the idea to lay down a track for Slagel's compilation, but they didn't have much time.

Regardless, Slagel and Kornarens went around collecting the fees from bands that wanted to appear on it. According to Tanner, a tune that later morphed into "Hit the Lights" was the one they talked about using, so they set about recording it. According to Tanner, the vibe in the sessions was good: "I had soccer practice one evening, but I called in afterward to see how rehearsals were going and Lars had definitely improved since James last saw him." The problem was that they needed a guitarist in order to get the track done in time.

The reason they needed a guitarist was that James was only playing bass and singing. McGovney—the logical choice to fill the bass player role—hadn't committed to joining the band full-time, although the other two were very keen for him to do so. Lars had a job at a gas station and James had a brief stint at a print shop, but neither was serious about those jobs and they were more into playing music.

Lars placed an ad in *Recycler* magazine and Lloyd Grant replied. Grant was one of the few black guitarists around the LA metal scene and he recalled getting together with Lars and James. "I answered an ad in the local paper that Lars placed," he told the author. "He auditioned several people and had the ad in there for a while."

Grant was one of numerous neighborhood people who had responded to the *Recycler* ad. Another was Joey Allen, who ended up as a guitarist in hair-metallers Warrant. Grant continued, "I got busy for a few weeks and then Lars got back in touch and played me James's tape of 'Hit the Lights.' I really liked it and it was the kind of stuff I wanted to do." Grant was pretty impressed by what he saw in Hetfield: "He was really good. Not quite as he is today but he was still very good. He was very quiet, though, and seemed quite shy."

Grant was in pole position for a permanent spot in the band, but there was another weird twist to come. Lars had left the *Recycler* ad running. McGovney recalled the phone call that he received as a result: "I took the call and all I remember is this guy on the other end and having to listen to him [talk] about himself. Then I called James to the phone and said, 'Here's another guitar player, but this guy's head won't fit through the door when he gets here.'"

The head in question belonged to Dave Mustaine, who had played with the Huntingdon Beach band Panic and had reason to be confident: he was something of a guitar hero with all manner of gear at his disposal. Having been in a functioning band, the confident Mustaine not only offered serious shredding ability. He also brought with him valuable live experience, which the others did not have.

Grant didn't help his own cause by not showing up to rehearsals sometimes. Grant said, "There are so many bands in LA and you never know whether they're going to make it. Also, you have to drive through traffic for rehearsals and I just didn't turn up sometimes. Then Dave came along and got in the band."

Mustaine did the two lead breaks intended for a version of "Hit the Lights," but the rest was Hetfield and Ulrich, as James told Metal Mike in an interview: "We borrowed ourselves a Tascam four-track and recorded 'Hit the Lights.' I played rhythm guitar and bass and sang, while Lars drummed. We were really a duo." Although Mustaine's two lead solos were adequate, a version of the second solo recorded by Grant—minutes before the tape was handed over to Slagel—was the one they went with.

Grant said there was no animosity after Mustaine replaced him. When asked the definitive reason for his departure, he responded, "You'll need to ask James and Lars that question." Grant and Lars still got along well enough to watch the 1982 World Cup Soccer matches together, and Grant has remained in touch with the band.

All that was needed now was to rush the track over to Slagel so that it could be mastered from reel-to-reel tape at Bijou Studios in Hollywood. However, Lars's recording was on a cassette tape and needed to be transferred.

Kornarens remembered the tape handover vividly. "The tape was due at 3:00 pm, and Brian and I are standing outside on the sidewalk, and this was busy Hollywood. Lars then comes running up all out of breath and pulls this cassette from his back pocket."

What Lars didn't know was that to convert the cassette to reel tape would cost $50, which he did not have. Kornarens recalled, "Lars's head all of a sudden turns to me and he says, 'Do you have fifty bucks?' Fortunately I had fifty-two bucks sitting in there, which I gave to him, and basically paid for the mastering of Metallica. I never got it back either!"

While the compilation was being finished, there were further developments within the band. James had used Ron McGovney's bass to record the bass parts for "Hit the Lights," but McGovney still wasn't keen on being a full-time band member. "I was more interested in going to see Mötley Crüe at the clubs," McGovney admitted. "Then one night we're sitting having a few beers and I start to play the bass part for 'Hit the Lights' and James, Lars and Dave join in. Maybe it was my drunkenness, or even my awe at Dave's guitar playing that made me finally agree to join."

When the track appeared on the first pressing of the *Metal Massacre* compilation, Metallica had a vinyl presence, which, rather unusually, preceded any recognized demo of their own. Amusingly, the first pressing had a few spelling errors, including Lloyd Grant's name and the band name, which read "Mettallica." While future pressings saw the errors corrected, that first edition remains a collector's item.

The origin of the band name has been the subject of considerable debate over the years. Tanner recalled hearing it from Lars and not being thrilled by it: "Honestly, like most names . . . I did not like it at first. No one else argued and it just came to pass. James had a draft board from his high school days and it was set up in Ron's house. James had already designed the Metallica logo on it, which is the logo exactly as it stands today."

Ron Quintana, the editor of a metal fanzine from San Francisco, had asked Ulrich which of two names, "Metallica" or "Metal Mania," sounded better for his fanzine. The Metallica name was taken for the band. Hetfield's early artistic ability, which had been shrewdly identified years ago by McGovney, turned out to be invaluable, as that logo is one of the most recognizable in music. Although the band abandoned it for a few album covers in the mid-1990s, the logo has remained largely the same to this day.

Another guy who recognized Hetfield's early talent was Katon De Pena, who formed the band Hirax. He recalled seeing the logo and was impressed: "James was extremely talented. Not just musically but artistically as well. I remember he showed me that hand-drawn logo and I remember thinking, *If this guy doesn't make it as a musician, he'll definitely make it as an artist.*" It wasn't just the band logo either, as Katon recalled: "He was always wearing T-shirts with all the newest kick-ass bands. One time he turned up in a Saxon *Strong Arm of the Law* shirt, which he made. And it was so good I was sure he must have got it from the Saxon fan-club, but he made it himself."

De Pena confirmed how initially reserved but ultimately likeable James was. "James was quiet, but once you got to know him he was great fun to hang out with. If you were into the same kind of music he was into . . . you could talk and get drunk for many, many hours! We all used to hang out together and do a bit of smoking and drinking. We'd always somehow end up listening to Diamond Head, Venom and Saxon albums. We'd rage all night until the sun came up, but every time, James would be the last one standing!"

With a band name and a track on a new compilation, the band—with a seemingly settled lineup—looked into playing live shows on the LA club circuit. What was still uncertain was whether James would be the band's full-time singer, which seems incredible when you consider how effective he has become.

Sammy DeJohn was an LA-based singer, whose path crossed with James during this period. "A couple of my friends were going to Hollywood to this little dive to see a band," DeJohn recalled. "They said I needed to see them. So we got to this bar and James is standing outside, so we walked up and started talking to him. He had this bottle of vodka so we took a couple of shots of that, and he told me they were looking for a singer."

James seemed keen to distance himself from vocal duties, even though the first song was out and was well received. "I ended up going down to their place to rehearse as their singer, and that lasted maybe a few weeks," DeJohn recalled. "But it never happened and I really don't think that Mustaine liked me at all." Despite the coalition not amounting to anything permanent, DeJohn recognized James's talent: "I thought James was really cool and we got along real well. As a musician, it's his voice and the way he totally commands the stage that makes him what he is."

The band members were regularly seen around the LA club scene. Bob Nalbandian, who ran a metal radio show in the area, remembered noticing James: "I saw him around the time they formed and it was out-side the Woodstock Club in Anaheim. There were two clubs next-door to each other—Woodstock and Radio City." Nalbandian, a regular in the rock and metal scene, turned up at the venues to see whatever band was playing. He said, "I would always see James at these shows and I never knew who he was. I used to have a jacket with Motörhead and Saxon patches on it and I'd always see James and he would always just stare at my jacket."

Despite clearly noticing Nalbandian and being intrigued by his clothing, Hetfield would rarely speak, as Nalbandian recalled: "He had a Motörhead shirt on back then and I was too shy to go up and talk to him either." Nalbandian had a friend named Pat Scott who had met Lars when he, too, responded to that famous *Recycler* ad, and that con-nection brought Lars into Nalbandian's world.

After a visit to Lars's house that involved raking through what Nalbandian described as "the ultimate record collection," he asked Scott if Lars was in a band. Scott replied, "Yeah, you know that guy we always see at the Woodstock with the Motörhead shirt? Well, he's the singer."

After that revelation, Nalbandian ran into Hetfield again at the Woodstock and this time they connected. Nalbandian recalled, "Finally he came up and I said, 'Hey! You're singing with that band Metallica, right?' And he freaked out and said, 'Wow, how do you know?' And then, 'Someone recognized me! We haven't even played a gig yet!' We started talking a bit and he was a really, really nice guy. He was real shy and quiet."

The two rapped about metal and all the cool bands in LA, not to mention Lars's record collection. "Lars was always the real driven one.

Back in the day James was real quiet and reserved," Nalbandian confirmed. "And the next time I would hang out with James would be after the band's first ever show at Radio City."

That legendary first live performance took place at Radio City on March 14, 1982, and from all reports, it was a total disaster. Nalbandian was there—as he was at all their early shows—and right from the get-go, things went hideously wrong. He explained: "It was horrible. Dave's guitar string broke and they didn't have a backup guitar, so in the middle of the set they had to restring it." Nalbandian remembered that the set list was pretty limited too: "They did just covers at the time and the only original was 'Hit the Lights' and maybe one other."

That disastrous debut didn't put the band off. Nalbandian recalled what Lars told him after the show: "Lars said, 'Yeah we're going to open up for Saxon in a couple of weeks.' And I said, 'Fuck you. You're full of shit. You'll never open for Saxon!' But they *did* get that show." The opportunity to open for Saxon at the Whisky came from McGovney's photography connections. His persistence put him in touch with the venue's booking agent. The second gig was apparently only a marginal improvement.

Nalbandian distinctly remembered how James behaved that night: "He was still very shy and he didn't talk to the audience at all. And you have to remember that he was only singing back then. It was only their second gig, and man, did it show."

Jim Durkin, a former student at Downey High School, was a few years younger than James. Durkin was an aspiring metal-head in those days and would eventually become part of the influential thrash outfit Dark Angel. He attended those early gigs, as he fondly recalled. "I'm not gonna say I was an old friend or anything and hung out all the time," Jim confessed, "but I was at all the gigs, and would go up and talk to James and Lars and ask questions—being the fan-boy I was. James gave me a Metallica button, which I still have."

Durkin had been learning guitar in his last year of high school, and he thought he knew a lot before he saw the band play. He said, "At the time I thought I knew what metal was. Then I met Dave Marrs, and he told me to go and see Metallica. I was blown away. It changed my life."

Tanner was still assisting the band. He was sniffing around trying to book live shows, recording time or anything else that would build the band's reputation. Tanner remembered how confident Lars was about his band making it big, particularly during one typically highly charged phone call. "We are going to be the world's greatest band and you are going to be the world's greatest manager," Ulrich yelled down the phone. He discussed two names that the management company could be called: Metal Up Your Ass Productions and Thunderfuck Productions.

While Tanner soon bowed out of the Metallica story, his role was very important. After being silent for so long, Tanner was keen that it should inspire young aspiring musicians: "All that I said was with the perspective of a high school kid longing to be a rock star. If this is you, then to you I dedicate my long-standing silence and wish you great success in your endeavors."

Looking to promote themselves following their early live exposure, the band put together a four-track demo. It consisted of "Hit the Lights," "Motorbreath," "Jump in the Fire" and "Mechanix"—which had been played at one of the band's early live shows. The cassette tape became known as *The Power Metal Demo.* That wasn't intentional, though. It only happened because McGovney had added the words "Power Metal" under the band's logo when he distributed the demo to club promoters in the area.

The Power Metal Demo was a stepping-stone to the band's first full demo, *No Life 'Til Leather* (the opening line of "Hit the Lights'). That demo included three newer songs: "Seek and Destroy," "Metal Militia" and "Phantom Lord."

De Pena, who was still part of James's social circle, remembers hearing the demo for the first time. "James made me sit down with old-school headphones and listen to it." He wouldn't be the only one compelled to hear this demo, if James got his way.

After raising some cash and going through a few creative differences with producer Kenny Kane, who had more of a punk reputation, the demo was recorded to everyone's satisfaction in a studio in Orange County. When it was released, it spread like wildfire—even as far afield as Japan. It got a rabid reception closer to home from a metal scene that was eager for something new.

There was great interest in San Francisco, LA's rival city six hours up the coast, which would become even more significant. Why did the demo make such a massive impact? That distinctive crunch in Hetfield's guitar sound forewarned what was to follow.

With his palm-muted picking, Hetfield had discovered a guitar sound that nobody had heard before—certainly not honed to this degree of precision and frightening power. Palm-muting is the practice of using the picking hand (in this case the right hand) to dampen the sound and not let it resonate. This gave metal riffs a new kind of blunt-force power, and young Hetfield was an early master.

Arguably, this was the beginning of thrash metal. Less palatable—and recognizable—was the vocal delivery, which had a more lightweight sound than latter-day Hetfield vocals. He was attempting to *sing* more here than in the clipped, barked delivery he'd famously adopt. James did not use much melody or harmony, so the vocals sounded rather immature at times. However, what James lacked vocally, he more than made up for with his guitar playing.

Jim Durkin, who was developing his own guitar playing, rated Hetfield among the greats. "Iommi invented the heavy sound, but James invented the thrash sound. Palm-muted and tight riffing. He was the law!"

Metallica played around the LA area, mixing with bands like Ratt and Stryper, with whom they had nothing in common in terms of sound or ideology. Slagel asked if the band would play on a bill called "Metal Massacre Night" at the Keystone in San Francisco on September 18, 1982. It was only because another band, Cirith Ungol, had dropped out that Metallica got the call, and that twist of fate forever altered the destiny of the band.

While things seemed to be rolling along nicely, a few differences surfaced among the band members, with McGovney feeling the pinch most. All bands' histories are full of rumors, but it's almost certain that Ron felt that his help, accommodation and general good nature were being taken for granted by the other three. This issue and further antagonism between bandmates were often fueled by alcohol, causing serious conflict between the band members.

When the time came to travel to San Francisco, McGovney used his dad's 1969 Ford Ranger to haul all the gear and his bandmates to a city he did not know his way around. He later told *Shockwaves* magazine that seeing his partying bandmates in the back of the van did little to relieve his frustration.

Something that must have softened the blow was the rabid response that greeted Metallica. Everyone who was there—and there were apparently only two hundred people at the show—said it was like a bomb had been dropped. As McGovney told KNAC, it was an eye-opener: "We had no idea our *No Life 'Til Leather* demo had gotten up there; they knew all the lyrics to our songs and everything." The Bay Area crowd understood where the band were coming from, as McGovney realized: "It was a trip; we couldn't believe it. When we played in LA with bands like Ratt, people would just stand there with their arms crossed."

James was still shy, Slagel recalled: "We all kind of traveled up together and stayed in the same hotel on that trip. He was still super shy, and he wasn't the kind of guy that you go and hang out with for hours on end and talk to him." Slagel added, "He was super-cool though, and obviously the more he drank, the more his personality came out in those days."

Despite that fantastic show, McGovney's position in the band was precarious for various reasons—some of them personal. His days in Metallica were numbered. "I was starting to feel alienated from the band. It was *them* and *me*," McGovney conceded. Relations were irreparable, and the band looked for a new bass player.

The McGovney situation was brought to Slagel's attention when they got together in LA. He suggested that they check out a Bay Area band called Trauma, whom he had seen at the Whisky a few weeks earlier. The point wasn't to see the band per se; Trauma included a bass player of astounding virtuosity, Cliff Burton.

Burton was like a whirlwind onstage. He was a talent that couldn't be ignored, in Slagel's educated opinion. McGovney remembered seeing Burton play with the others and viewed that night as a death sentence for him in the band: "I remember saying to James: 'That bass player is playing the lead!' He and Lars were mesmerized. I thought, 'Oh, no, here is the end.'"

Never one to miss an opportunity, Lars approached Burton after the show with an offer to join the band. He was surprised when Burton declined because of his feelings about LA. Nevertheless, from that day on, Cliff Burton was going to be the next Metallica bass player.

Metallica continued to play live shows despite feeling that they were never accepted by an LA crowd that preferred glam and hair metal. Ironically, thrash was starting to catch on in LA when Metallica were about to leave. As Durkin recalled: "At the start there were no bands anywhere near that sound in LA. Then all of a sudden, bands started popping up all over LA, doing their own take on things—including Dark Angel."

Durkin wasn't convinced that Metallica invented thrash. "Metallica opened the door, opened eyes. There was more to the local metal scene than just being the next Maiden, Priest or Sabbath. Did they invent thrash? No, that sound was defined by all the bands to come, but Metallica certainly set the standard."

Despite declining Lars's offer, Burton remained in the picture and even attended an October show at the Old Waldorf. The band's performance was well received—at least by LA standards.

November saw another breakthrough performance at the Woodstock in Anaheim, where Metallica supported journeyman metal act Y&T. Previously Metallica only had one guitar at live shows, and Nalbandian remembered the impact of James playing a second guitar that night: "It really beefed up their sound, and that was a turning point where I thought, *Wow, this band could really do something*, because until then they had never really gone down that well."

The next two shows the band played were vital. The show on November 29 at the Old Waldorf was recorded for live demo purposes. It was released under the name *Live Metal Up Your Ass*. Due to problems with the venue's mixing board, the show was recorded via a cassette recorder placed in front of the PA. The sound quality was hideous. In addition, the support band was an up-and-coming Bay Area group called Exodus. Their guitarist was a shy twenty-year-old named Kirk Hammett—but more on him later.

The next night, Metallica played their second show in San Francisco at the Mabuhay Gardens. It was the last time McGovney played with the band. The return trip down the coast was a culmination of everything that was bad about his relationship with his colleagues. McGovney had had enough, as he recalled: "Cliff was at that gig in San Francisco and for me the writing was on the wall. So when we got back to LA, I quit." Friction between McGovney and Mustaine exacerbated matters, and McGovney kicked everyone out of his house.

Burton finally agreed to join the band. Burton was thoughtful and wise beyond his years. While he was fond of partying, he wasn't boisterous or loud. He had a wealth of talent and an implacable will for where it might take him. That drive became a valuable addition to the tapestry of Metallica.

McGovney conceded that the band was not everything for him: "I admit I spent more time with my girlfriend than with those other guys. This was my first girlfriend, you know, a hot chick to spend quality time with. I also missed a few band practices to go and see Mötley Crüe gigs, and they didn't like that at all."

Without McGovney, the James Hetfield story would have been very different. Without a place to live and practice, Hetfield's adolescent life may have progressed very differently. Nalbandian summed it up well: "I always say this about Ron: he was an integral part of the early days of Metallica."

McGovney looked at it more modestly: "I think they would have found a way. I think that Lars can talk anyone into anything. He is just so persistent and they definitely had the drive and talent to make it without my financial support." A classy sign-off from a classy guy.

At this point McGovney exited the James Hetfield story, and Metallica soon departed an ungrateful Los Angeles for a receptive San Francisco.

CHAPTER 4
THE METALLICA MANSION AND THE MUSIC BUILDING

With the drama surrounding McGovney's departure behind them, Hetfield, Ulrich and Mustaine now had to figure out how to move all their belongings to San Francisco, which took almost four months to complete. It wouldn't be until late March 1983 that James and Lars would take up residence at 3132 Carlson Boulevard in El Cerrito, which belonged to a friend named Mark Whitaker. The apartment was a little run-down, and the neighborhood was not one of the area's best. The residence got the rather ironic nickname The Metallica Mansion.

Ron Quintana was invited to a few of the many early parties that took place at the Mansion. "James was very gruff. Very withdrawn and hidden," he recalled. "Until he drank, then he'd kind of come out of his shell." Whitaker was training to become a sound engineer as well as managing Exodus, with whom Metallica had played a show at the tail end of 1982. Mustaine took a room at Whitaker's grandmother's house, which must have been a strange mixture—but it seemed to work. Although it took a while, the move was worth doing, as James told *Thrasher* magazine in 1986: "Now that I think of it . . . it was really wild that we did that. All of a sudden, we just move up to SF, no place to stay or nothing. It was cool!"

In the early 1980s, the Bay Area had a fast, evolving, vibrant metal scene. The musicians in the scene were very tight, which meant they congregated at the same gigs and parties. The main players in the early days were Metallica and Exodus, but there was a host of other bands, like Death Angel and Possessed, on the rise. They were spurred on by an energy and atmosphere that suggested something serious was in the air.

It wasn't a big scene geographically, and the club circuit revolved around venues like Ruthie's Inn, The Waldorf, the Stone and Mabuhay Gardens. What they lacked in size and number, the clubs made up for in energy. These sweaty venues seemed to inhale the sound that the bands emitted. On any given night you could see four or five killer bands perform on the same bill.

A Bay Area resident named Fred Cotton ran into James after one of the shows at the Stone. Hetfield had a lot in common with him and he became an important ally for several years. Fred recalled: "We went to a party back at Mark Whitaker's and we totally hit it off. He had a presence about him definitely, but I had no idea at that time that he'd become what he did. At that time, he just looked like someone you'd want to hang out and identify with."

Cotton noticed that something was going on in the Bay Area music scene. He explained, "At the time; they were *it*. That was the shit. I mean, I was floored. James really connected with the people through the music just by being himself. The music back then was so amazing—all you could do was just bow."

This was a new movement, but the area had long been receptive to metal. Eric Peterson, who founded Legacy (Testament's early incarnation), grew up in the Bay Area and remembered his early exposure to metal fondly: "When I was fifteen or sixteen the Bay Area had this thing called 'Day on the Green' at the outdoor Coliseum. Every summer we had two of them. My first concert was Ted Nugent, Aerosmith, AC/DC with Bon Scott and Mahogany Rush."

Peterson's future bandmate, who was also part of the scene, was Chuck Billy. Billy became the singer of Testament, a band that followed in the Metallica slipstream and released their first—and arguably best—record in 1987. Although Testament didn't achieve the vast commercial success that Metallica did, the band remains an important player in the genre.

Billy is a larger-than-life character and one of the most respected guys in the music business. He vividly remembered James in the early days in San Francisco. "Metallica actually bonded that scene together even tighter. James was always the guy who was just real and never beat around the bush. He was kind of loud and outspoken back then with a little more drinking and partying than nowadays maybe," Billy said. "So it was a different James back then."

The presence of Metallica was a unifying factor for the Bay Area thrash scene. The band did their part to support other acts who were fighting to make their way, as Billy recalled: "When we started, James and the other guys would always come down to our shows and that was a big highlight for us. And it also made us be on our toes!"

Quintana, who was running a radio station, recalled that James used to guest DJ on his show, with mixed results: "[Metallica] would come up and guest DJ, or instead come on and be drunk and swear—getting me in trouble!" It wasn't all about partying for Metallica, though. With Burton now onboard, Metallica capitalized on the excitement that their *No Life 'Til Leather* demo had generated and built on their already excellent reputation for live performances. Many early witnesses opined that the Metallica sound took on a new dimension with Burton's classically trained playing, and the live Metallica experience benefited from his energetic stage presence.

At one gig at the Stone in the spring of 1983, the band added some more complex features to their live experience, most notably a Burton bass solo called "Anesthesia" along with a couple of new and reworked songs.

The West Coast wasn't the only place that the Metallica effect was felt. Three time zones away, the roughly recorded *Live Metal Up Your Ass* demo had found its way into the hands of an artist manager and record store entrepreneur named Jon Zazula, nicknamed Jonny Z.

Zazula had a famous record store called Rock 'n' Roll Heaven, which was located in East Brunswick, New Jersey. He and his wife, Marsha, managed bands under the name Crazed Management, and they were both renowned for their ability to spot new talent and develop it to maximum commercial effect. Their foresight and persistence had successfully introduced metal bands like Anvil and Venom to an American audience.

Jonny was an extrovert who'd approach every project with total enthusiasm and determination. What the Zazulas saw in Metallica was an energy and newness that blended the sound of bands like Motörhead and the NWOBHM with something very American. In their eyes, this was an innovative, lethal and potentially lucrative combination.

Zazula recalled hearing the demo: "Somebody brought the demo into the store and it blew my mind. I thought this was the greatest thing since white bread. Marsha and I had twelve shows going on at the time with bands like Twisted Sister and we thought it would be cool to bring them [Metallica] over and give them a shot."

Impressed by what they heard, the Zazulas told Ulrich that they'd like the band to come to New York, play shows and talk about some business ideas. Lars knew the Zazulas' reputation for being shrewd judges of talent, so he agreed to travel over with the band.

The only problem was that they didn't have any money. Zazula sent them $1,500 towards the cost of the trip. "To me [that] was like a million dollars back then," he said. The band, accompanied by Whitaker, rented a U-Haul van and a truck.

What occurred on that 3,000-mile journey was infamous. The close confines of a long-distance trip brought matters to a head. According to rumors, James and Lars had already made the decision to kick Mustaine out of the band at a point "somewhere between Chicago and Idaho," but they did not do it officially until they got to the East Coast.

Zazula recalled the band arriving at his home: "When they got to my house, two of them had been in the back of the truck the whole ride with the gear, and the other three were in the front." Zazula was surprised by what happened next: "The first thing they did after 'hello' was to raid my liquor cabinet!"

What became apparent was that they didn't have anywhere else to go. "They had nothing except the gear and the clothes on their back,"

Zazula confirmed. For the first part of the trip, the band continued to stay at the Zazulas' house as guests, until an alternative was available.

Although Mustaine hadn't officially left yet, the band had a contingency plan to replace him, and the person they had in mind was Exodus guitarist Kirk Hammett. They'd become aware of his ability through San Francisco metal circles and Whitaker managed Hammett's band, so there was an open channel of communication.

In New York, Metallica played live shows on April 8 and 9, supporting Vandenberg and the Rods, respectively. After a day off they packed Mustaine's bags for him, and Hetfield told him he was no longer in the band. As the story goes, there was very little discussion or ceremony, and Mustaine was on a Greyhound bus back to San Francisco one hour later. Whatever the reasons were, Dave Marrs believed Mustaine would have been fired at some point later if not then: "I just don't think they ever would have got along. I really don't." The Metallica vs. Mustaine debate rumbled on for years, and of all the band members, Hetfield probably commented about it the least. To this day, it is a subject that fans of Metallica regularly bring up.

Mustaine went on to form Megadeth—a monster act in their own right. Throughout their extremely successful career, Megadeth contributed hugely to the fabric of rock music. Many experts considered their 1990 album, *Rust in Peace*, one of the best technical metal albums.

A call was put in to Hammett asking him to fly to New York immediately to audition for a spot in Metallica. The timing was good because Hammett liked what he had seen of Metallica and was frustrated with Exodus's lack of progress. It suited both parties, and despite Hammett thinking that the initial call was a hoax, he flew to New York.

When Hammett arrived, he started jamming with Hetfield, Ulrich and Burton. He played brilliantly and so was in the band. Hammett made his live debut with Metallica on April 16 at the Showplace in New Jersey.

Metallica continued to party hard at the Zazula residence, and John and Marsha decided they should go elsewhere. The Zazulas found them accommodation in a place called The Music Building in Queens, New York. That would have been fine if there had been any rooms left, as Zazula recalled: "We found them a terrible place! They were living in squalor at the top of the building where all the garbage was kept. Things like old desks and chairs were in there instead of being thrown out in the street." Also using that building was the thrash band Anthrax, who were from Queens and had a room set up there to rehearse.

Anthrax became the East Coast wing of the so-called "Big Four" of thrash bands, with the other three being Megadeth, Slayer and of course Metallica. Their career ran fairly parallel to Metallica's until the early 1990s, but thereafter Metallica ascended into rock superstardom while Anthrax settled into a relatively low profile. The bands were very close in those early days. Anthrax's drummer, Charlie Benante, recalled when James and the boys showed up: "I met James for the first time at our rehearsal studio and that's where the friendship started. For me, I bonded most with Kirk at first. James was kind of quiet in the beginning. I always felt in the early days that James was quite un-approachable. And then once the surface stuff was finished, we could kind of hang and talk about shit."

Benante confirmed an impression of Hetfield that many people shared, and apparently it took him a while to let his guard down.

Maybe it was shyness, or maybe it was a general mistrust of people that dated back to his childhood in Downey.

Hetfield was a tough nut to crack, as even Zazula admitted: "It took a bit to get to talk to him personally from what I remember. You had to catch James at the right moment. It seemed in those days that he carried a lot of ghosts, and he certainly didn't like to discuss them. But I guess if you want to get personal with a person, you ask those questions, but he wasn't so quick to give up the answers." That summation of the Hetfield psyche is as good a marker as any for where he was at age twenty. Zazula's references to "ghosts" surely referred to James's pain and lack of understanding from his parents' divorce and his mother's premature death.

James was becoming increasingly dominant in the lineup. There were two quiet and relatively mild figures in Hammett and Burton. There was the confident and super-energetic Ulrich. And then there was the passively controlling specter of Hetfield. This triangle of power and control probably started when Hammett joined. This period—prior to any full album—marks the beginning of many years of tension, which at times led to tremendous creativity and at other times threatened to destroy the band.

The benefits of being under the Zazulas' wing were obvious. The next live gigs organized were an act of genius on Jon Zazula's part. He paired Metallica with legendary British black metal pioneers Venom. The two shows the bands played at the Paramount on Staten Island on April 22 and 24, 1983, went down in metal history—albeit not for the right reasons.

Observers would have put Venom at the evil end of the metal spectrum. With two well-received albums and a reputation for insane live shows, they were a few steps ahead of Metallica. Like Metallica previously, Venom was invited to reside at the Zazula house ahead of the shows. What actually happened is probably best left to the imagination, but on one occasion the Zazulas' kitchen apparently nearly caught fire after a late night cooking attempt.

Venom didn't reserve their fiery exploits for the Zazulas' kitchen. They almost destroyed the Paramount on the first night due to an ambitious pyrotechnic display. Hetfield got caught up in the excitement of those Venom shows, and it cost him a trip to the hospital to treat six stitches in his hand after falling while holding a vodka bottle.

Despite all the drama, the combination of Metallica and their heroes Venom on the same bill was considered a complete success by all concerned, particularly James and Lars, who told a KUSF interviewer: "We might do something with Venom if they can get off their ass and do more than one album every five years."

After seeing Metallica's potential, Zazula considered finding a way to record the band's debut album. Although he was not officially their manager, Zazula had taken on a surrogate role that worked for both parties. In any case, the band had no viable alternatives back in San Francisco.

There were two problems. First, no record companies gave a damn about being involved with Metallica or had any desire to take a commercial risk on a relatively extreme act. Second, even if a company had wanted a piece of Metallica, the band had no financial muscle, which meant that any album deal would need to be done on a minimal budget.

What the Zazulas did next was one of the most risky yet shrewd decisions in rock history. Zazula recalled, "We decided that we should fund the whole damn thing ourselves. The recording, the manufacturing, everything."

CHAPTER 5
KILL 'EM ALL

Getting a raw entity like Metallica to record an album was an achievement that cannot be underestimated, especially given the minimal resources available. The Zazulas had just had a child, and putting themselves out there financially was extremely risky. To pull it off, they needed everything to fall right. Fortunately, due to the togetherness that only regular live shows can bring, the band were in good shape to proficiently lay down tracks in a studio situation. Just as well, given that the Zazulas couldn't afford much time.

Anthrax's Charlie Benante, having seen Hetfield sing firsthand, knew what his strengths were: "James just went up there and said, '*This is how I'm going to sing, you can either love it or hate it.*' Luckily for him, it went well with the music. Just like Lemmy goes well with Motörhead's music."

None of this uncertainty worried Zazula, as his determined approach had already hooked him up with a recording studio in upstate New York called Barren Alley. By the time Metallica turned up during the first week of May, the studio was called Music America.

Zazula remembered that it was easily the best option available: "It had a really good sound board and there was a good space where you could crash. It was a good, clean, big studio and Manowar had just recorded there. Manowar sounded really good to us for those days, and we're talking about *Into Glory Ride*, not the other album."

Zazula found a recording space as well as a sound engineer named Chris Bubacz who, as he said, "seemed to get it." Also available was Paul Curcio, who had the unenviable task of faithfully committing Metallica's live sound to vinyl for the first time.

"Paul was a big guitar guy, and I believe he worked on some of the early Santana albums. He really understood the guitar, although he didn't really understand the heaviness of it," Zazula explained. Curcio was quickly educated as to what the band wanted, and within a couple of weeks, ten tracks were recorded.

Zazula particularly remembered a unique ability of Hetfield's during that recording process: "I thought of James as an artist with a talent. Except his way of painting was by heavying songs up. On one occasion while we were recording *Kill 'Em All*, James came up to me and said, 'Hey, do I get to heavy my album up yet?'" When the album was recorded, it apparently had a lot of high-end guitar and was distinctly lightweight in sound—until James was asked to go back into the studio and change that.

As far as the title was concerned, James and the band wanted to name the record *Metal Up Your Ass*. Zazula and the distribution company felt that something so direct and visceral (the cover would have had an image of a sword emerging from a toilet bowl) wouldn't fly in a cautious music business. The band didn't like that prudent approach. As the story goes, Burton suggested the title *Kill 'Em All* in reference to what he'd like to do to record label types—and everyone immediately agreed.

The album cover was a blunt statement of intent, depicting a large, heavy-looking hammer, a pool of blood, and the ominous shadow of the hand that was presumably wielding the hammer. It was "no-nonsense" and represented the record's content well.

The album's ten tracks had all been played live at some point during the previous year. Some of them dated back even further. It was a potent selection of songs that sounded like nothing else out there. While the recording process was largely successful—in that the result was a stunning debut—there is some debate as to whether the band were happy with how much help they got during the two weeks it took to lay the album down.

Given that it was his baby, Zazula was understandably defensive: "Paul Curcio was definitely told what was required and I don't remember James complaining." Hetfield was a lot more direct when asked about the sessions by *Thrasher* magazine in 1986. He was openly critical of Curcio.

So, what of the album itself? To critically assess a record that is intrinsic to the fabric of what we know as heavy metal is like a modern art critic attempting to sensibly appraise the *Mona Lisa*. It's no easy job. With that proviso in mind, the record fades straight into "Hit the Lights," which had been around in some form or another for at least five years. This version is a far more streamlined beast, which illustrates how far the new lineup had come. What is immediately apparent is the utter precision and speed of Hetfield's rhythm attack—which of course is key in order for music played at this velocity to be effective. The remainder of the record is equally effective.

With the album recorded and being pressed to appear on the Zazulas' new label, Megaforce, Metallica went out on the road with another British power metal band called Raven, with whom Zazula had already forged links. The tour, entitled the Kill 'Em All for One tour (Raven's new album was called *All for One*) kicked off on the East Coast. It then went through various parts of the country en route to a finale in California in early September.

This was the band's first full tour of any great duration, and in an interview with Metal Mike of *Aardschok*, Hetfield admitted that it was a struggle at times: "There were really horrible smells on that bus, as there was a lot of drinking, puking and fucking going on. You would have to get drunk to actually fall asleep on that thing as it was so horrible . . . halfway through Texas the air-conditioning system broke, and it was like traveling in an oven. You woke up in the morning and your tongue was stuck to your palate, because it was two hundred degrees in there!"

Heat wasn't the only issue. That tour had a reputation for being one of the most debauched metal tours ever. The fact that the two bands were living on top of one another in a bus, combined with furious alcohol consumption, stoked an already incendiary combination.

Despite riotous offstage behavior, the tour went extremely well and Metallica grew considerably as a band. The same could not be said for Raven, however, who sometimes struggled to appeal to Metallica's audience.

David Ellefson—the bass player in Megadeth, the thrash outfit Mustaine formed after his departure from Metallica—remembered running into James outside an LA venue on that Raven tour: "I had no history with James at that time and had recently relocated from the Midwest myself. I really liked their music and their band, though."

Ellefson had recently met Mustaine and joined his band, so he clearly felt he was in a strange position with the Metallica guys: "My involvement with James was mostly on a peer-to-peer, musician-to-musician type level, and I sometimes wondered whether I should be in opposition to them."

Ellefson, one of rock's most intelligent commentators, described an interesting if predictable contradiction that Hetfield presented in those days: "For a guy who had such a huge presence onstage and roars like a lion when he's singing, when he's off the stage I found him to be very introverted, and not someone who was overly animated at all. I actually admired that quality in him."

Ellefson confirmed a lot of what was known about Hetfield's persona. He said, "I get it. Obviously his stage persona is genuine. You *can* be one guy off the stage, but when you put your guitar on and saddle up, it's almost like you're walking out of a telephone booth in *Superman*—this other guy appears."

Ellefson recognized what was happening in the metal scene when he saw Metallica at The Country Club in LA. "They basically played songs as I knew them on the record, and I thought they were fantastic. You could definitely tell this was a movement." Ellefson noticed that despite being the focal person in the band, Hetfield wasn't comfortable with a role that involved talking to the audience between songs. Ellefson explained, "He just shut up and played, which I thought was kind of cool. He didn't try and get a reaction, he let his music get the reaction, and I admired that."

Bob Nalbandian was also at that show, and he was impressed by how Metallica had improved. "That show was the first time I'd seen them with Kirk in the band and they fucking just blew me away. It wasn't just Kirk—because I actually preferred Dave Mustaine—it was just James's professionalism that was most amazing. He'd also become so much more confident."

The debut album was released while the band were on tour, and album sales were frenetic. By the end of 1983, *Kill 'Em All* had shifted an impressive 17,000 copies in the United States alone. In order to capitalize on wider interest in the band, Zazula teamed up with Martin Hooker in the UK, who had a vague knowledge of the band after hearing the *No Life 'Til Leather* demo earlier.

Hooker had just founded his own record company in 1982 called Music for Nations. He was on the lookout for new opportunities when a copy of *Kill 'Em All* landed on his desk, and it checked all the right boxes. Zazula and Hooker immediately bonded, and a three-album contract gave Music for Nations responsibility for Metallica's releases in the UK and Europe.

Getting Metallica across to the UK and European audience was quite a challenge, particularly as the UK only received 1,300 copies of the album at the outset. However, following a successful club tour, the live Metallica experience pricked the ears of the metal public and album sales escalated rapidly. Zazula remembered with amusement the reaction of some of the A&R people he took the album to: "Most of them didn't have a clue what was going on."

By late 1983, the band were back in San Francisco enjoying the perks that their newfound fame afforded—which involved partying and drinking furiously with anyone who'd join them. One band that was more than willing to get involved was Armored Saint from LA, who had been signed to Brian Slagel's Metal Blade label, with whom the band played a live show in November 1983.

Apparently, vast drinking sessions ensued, culminating in Hetfield throwing beer bottles and other items out of a hotel room window and into the swimming pool. A trip to retrieve a leather jacket resulted in elevator doors being opened by Hetfield between floors, followed by soaking guests with a fire extinguisher. The live shows (including a few with Zazula's new Megaforce recruits Anthrax) didn't suffer—and the band continued to grow as a unit, with Hetfield coming out of his shell as a front man.

Although *Kill 'Em All* had only been out a matter of months, Metallica—or more specifically Hetfield—were already giving considerable thought to writing new material. The last gigs the band played that year included one or two new tracks that would appear on the next album. Audiences who heard the new songs were surprised by the band's step forward with songwriting. The new material was destined to change *everything*.

CHAPTER 6
1984 AND BEYOND

When 1984 rolled around, it was less Orwellian than some had predicted. Far from being a time of media censorship and cultural repression, there was an outburst of aural productivity, and it was an exciting time to be a metal-head. In many ways, 1984 was a pivotal year in the genre. Some of the more established bands enjoyed career-high success, while new acts—including Metallica—were trying to crash the party.

Iron Maiden, the most successful act to hail from the NWOBHM that Lars loved so much, released their mighty Egyptian-themed *Powerslave* that year, while Judas Priest—that other force of British metal—were flying high with *Defenders of the Faith*. Both bands continued to tour and release quality material for another twenty-five–plus years, but this was one of several peaks for both bands, particularly Iron Maiden. Their vast stage sets and ambitious visual production set the standard for any rock band to follow.

The Swiss band Celtic Frost—who influenced a slew of black metal and death metal bands with their off-kilter and avant-garde debut, *Morbid Tales*—were another young act trying to break into the market with a much darker and extreme sound.

With a growing number of likeminded followers in Europe, if ever there was an opportunity for Metallica to establish themselves at the forefront of a transient metal scene, 1984 was it.

The year did not begin exactly as planned. After a gig at the Channel Club in Boston on January 14, Metallica's gear was stolen from a van outside the venue. Hetfield felt the loss of equipment more than most apparently, as he'd become reliant on a particular Marshall amplifier to create the guitar sound he wanted. Borrowed equipment from fellow Zazula-managed act Anthrax was a suitable replacement and allowed Metallica to finish the tour.

There was no letup despite losing equipment. The Zazulas mined their new relationship with Venom further by booking Metallica to tour Europe with Venom on the Seven Dates of Hell tour. Dave Marrs, whose involvement with Hetfield dated back to their school days in Downey, was still working for the band as Lars's drum roadie and remembered this Venom tour as a turning point: "We listened to Mercyful Fate pretty much 24/7 on that tour on the bus as I recall, and then when we were in Denmark and we went to Sweet Silence Studios, the band were actually there. At that point they didn't have enough money to keep me in Europe so I had to come home. I don't really feel any regrets, though, as I didn't really know what the hell I was doing up there. When you go out on the road you find out real quick whether it's meant for you or not, and it just wasn't meant for me."

Another of the important figures in Hetfield's early life left the story. As with Hugh Tanner before him, life in a metal band wasn't the right career path. Marrs, like Tanner and McGovney, was a key link back to the early days in Downey and his departure left Hetfield on his own with the band.

Just as they had on the US tour with Venom the previous year, Metallica went "fuckin' nuts on the first night," as Venom guitarist Jeff Dunn bluntly described it. The two bands had serious chemistry, and that led to debauched drinking and chaos that continued until the tour finale at the Aardschock Festival in Holland on February 12.

In the festival crowd that day was German metal fan Mille Petrozza, who went on to form an uncompromising thrash band called Kreator. They would become one of Europe's premier thrash flag-bearers during the 1980s and refused to change their style in the lean days of the 1990s, when thrash was driven largely underground.

Petrozza remembered being inspired by Hetfield and Metallica even before that Aardschock appearance: "When *Kill 'Em All* came out, it was like some kind of sonic revolution. There were bands out there like Venom and Accept that played fast, but Metallica took this style to a level of perfection." When discussing that day in Holland, Petrozza was equally reverential: "We were excited when we heard that they would open for Venom and everyone went there to see Metallica. It was an experience I'll never forget."

Dunn acknowledged the success of the tour and recalled how the bands interacted: "Lars was always the spokesperson and always had the most to say. James was always down-to-earth, just a genuinely nice guy who seemed to be pleased to be there and was there for the love of it."

Metallica, Hooker and Music for Nations gave serious thought to the second Metallica album. They released "Jump in the Fire" from *Kill 'Em All* as a single, along with live versions of "Seek and Destroy" and "Phantom Lord." It was a stopgap release, but one that sustained fans' attention until new material was ready.

Instead of returning to America to record, the band remained in Europe—in Lars's home country of Denmark. The responsibility of following up *Kill 'Em All* from behind the mixing desk went to the calm Danish producer Flemming Rasmussen, whose Sweet Silence Studios became the band's home for the next few weeks.

Rasmussen was an easygoing guy who'd come to the band's attention on the back of British traditional rock band Rainbow's *Difficult to Cure*, to which he'd given an energetic gloss in 1981. Given that he'd dealt with Rainbow's mix of egos and personalities, he was the ideal choice on both an interpersonal and sonic level.

Metallica did not want a repeat of the *Kill 'Em All* sessions, where they felt they could have had more help from their producer. What they needed was someone who could refine or, even better, develop the band's sound, and with Rasmussen they felt they had the right man. The fact that this was Lars's hometown was also significant, as it served as a safety blanket for the band. Because it had taken all the available funds to get the band into the studio, they made full use of those facilities by sleeping there, too—they couldn't afford hotel rooms.

According to Marrs, after the Venom tour ended in February, the band drove to Sweet Silence, which had recently been used by Mercyful Fate and their charismatic singer, King Diamond. Album number two was called *Ride the Lightning*, and the road to making it happen began and ended at Sweet Silence.

Rasmussen recalled, "The first time I met [Hetfield] was in the studio, and he's got a pretty strong mind about what he wants from a sound perspective." There was an immediate problem: Hetfield's favorite guitar amp had disappeared at that Boston show. Hetfield and Rasmussen had to put their heads together to arrive at a solution, as Rasmussen recalled: "We started out playing some *Kill 'Em All* tracks so I could hear what he was talking about, and we started testing guitar amps, which took a couple of days."

The original amp had been modified, which meant, as Rasmussen bluntly stated: "Nobody remembered what the fuck had gone on, so we were all kind of lost. What we ended up with was something very different, which from my point of view was brilliant because I could then work on getting the sounds I wanted."

Even at this early stage, Hetfield had developed a unique guitar sound, and it took Rasmussen to make the best of James's newfound need to sound like nobody else on the planet. Rasmussen explained, "He liked the fact that he had his own sound and wasn't trying to copy someone else's. I think we took most of the recording process to pretty much get his thing. So we ended up looking for something that was new but also sounded something like his own stolen amp." But what did the Dane make of the man on a personal level? "I always considered James to be an angry young man. He had a great attitude I thought, though."

Rasmussen was the perfect foil for the opinionated Hetfield back in1984. He tempered Hetfield's angst and channeled those feelings down a creative route. The *Ride the Lightning* sessions under

Rasmussen's care might have been the beginning of a more musically mature James Hetfield.

The business acumen of Hetfield was also put to the test, as Rasmussen noticed: "They were negotiating a new deal because they were on that independent [Megaforce] label. They had different conversations with various labels and he was a big part of that. He's a smart guy."

The recording process was split into two chunks: February/March and part of June. During the break in between, the band headed to London to play two shows at the renowned Marquee Club. This kept the pot boiling for a UK audience, who were well aware that a new record was imminent.

Originally, Metallica were scheduled to tour Europe with two other Megaforce acts, The Rods and Exciter, but the Hell on Earth Tour had to be scrapped—rumored to be due to poor ticket sales. Dan Beehler, the drummer and vocalist with Canadian thrashers Exciter, recalled an encounter with James in London around that time. "Music for Nations rented two apartments in Baker Street; Metallica were in the basement and we were above," Beehler said. "I would go down and hang out with James and the boys, and we'd party large."

Beehler recalled being somewhat surprised by Hetfield's stature: "When I first saw the back of the *Kill 'Em All* album cover, I thought he was a little guy. Then when I met him he was pretty tall. He's a super guy and was totally happy-go-lucky and loved to have a good time back then."

Metallica returned to Copenhagen and put the album to bed. Afterward they went on a brief four-date tour with New York grease-paint rockers Twisted Sister, finishing on June 10.

On June 27, *Ride the Lightning* landed with an almighty thud. Zazula released it on Megaforce in the US, had Music for Nations do the honors in the UK and negotiated for a label called Roadrunner to handle it in Holland.

The response across the board was one of open-mouthed disbelief. *Kill 'Em All* was an aggressive, heavy affair and a fabulous debut, but *Ride the Lightning* was a huge step forward. The growth in both sound and songwriting was so marked that one could be forgiven for questioning if this was the same band. Hetfield's contribution had morphed from being, in retrospect, an awkward debut into a far more dominant role, in terms of both his vocals and his rhythm guitar precision.

Rasmussen captured the band's heaviness yet found a way to give that sound space to breathe—all with devastating effect. When asked in 1988 about the way *Ride the Lightning* sounded, Hetfield bluntly stated, "Flemming was in a reverb daze." The album did have a lot of reverb, but nobody could question the songs.

Even the front cover—which depicted an electric chair suspended in what looked like a night sky, beneath that now familiar logo—was a more mature statement of the band's rapid growth.

As opening tracks go, "Fight Fire with Fire" was one of Metallica's most telling compositions ever. Note the word "composition" because one of *Ride the Lightning*'s most impressive features was its implacable will to create complex yet powerful songs. Previous material had been delivered much more crudely.

Starting with a delicate but highly ominous acoustic intro, the track festers into a terrifying fade-in that in turn heralds a riff of warp-speed brutality. The song signs off with the sound of a nuclear explosion that leads directly into the title track, with no discernable pause for breath. Its whining dual guitar intro settles into a mid-tempo chug, with

Hetfield taking on the role of a condemned man awaiting his electric chair fate. The music is complex, taking in a progressive midsection and a stirring Hammett guitar solo, before returning to where it began.

For many, the focal point of *Ride the Lightning* is the penultimate track, the unforgettable "Creeping Death." Kicking in with a monstrous, repeated guitar salvo, it eases into a fluidly effective riff. The lyrics deal with "The Tale of the Firstborn" from the Book of Exodus. "Creeping Death" encompasses everything that the band was about at the time, and it became the most frequently played live song in the band's career.

While the excitement about the album release was raging, there was a management issue to resolve and a tour to embark on. Metallica's relationship with the enthusiastic and extremely generous Zazulas and Megaforce was running out of time. Without them the band might not have ever released an album, but Metallica had outgrown Megaforce. The band needed the support of a big label to make good on the huge potential suggested by *Ride the Lightning*.

Zazula concurred with that theory: "It was really in the band's best interest to move on. In those days it actually meant something to be on a record label."

The switch to a major label was in the works, and a New Yorker named Michael Alago had already taken small steps to make it happen. Alago noted, "I had started working for the Elektra label in March of 1983, and my job was to sign and develop new artists."

Zazula's and Alago's paths had already crossed, given that Raven were signed to Megaforce and Alago was involved with recording demos for them. Receiving a copy of *Kill 'Em All* changed everything for Alago. He recalled, "It slayed me. So one day I flew to San Francisco to see the band and they just fucking blew me away. I knew right then that these people were extraordinary."

Although the affable and outgoing Alago spoke to Ulrich that night and made the band aware of who he was, he had to wait until the summer of 1984 to take further action. Alago was immediately impressed by what he saw in Hetfield, even after only one meeting: "I saw James as a natural-born leader and a real wild child as a performer. He was one of the best even in those early days."

Zazula and Megaforce organized a showcase gig for their acts on August 3, at the Roseland in New York, consisting of Metallica, Anthrax and Raven. It proved to be a memorable night for several reasons, not least of all because several observers suggested Metallica put their label-mates to the sword. Alago recalled, "That night belonged to Metallica and the energy in the air was electric. They performed brilliantly and I was just so amped by what I saw."

Alago wasn't the only industry heavyweight there. Also impressed by the Metallica experience was Cliff Burnstein, the cofounder of an artist management company called Q Prime. Burnstein and Q Prime soon became a significant part of Metallica's world, and Alago was keen that the band become a part of his too. He recalled, "I ran backstage that night and practically barricaded the door shut, while I told them how much I loved them and wanted them in my personal and business world."

Whatever Alago imparted while locked in Metallica's dressing room must have worked. "The next day they came by the Elektra offices and we got some Chinese food and some beers, and the rest is history. You better believe it!" he recounted with considerable pride.

Within a couple of days, Metallica signed contracts with Q Prime and then with Elektra. Although the Elektra deal was not necessarily the best available financially, the band recognized the label's reputation for giving artists creative freedom. Heavy metal—or, more specifically, thrash metal—was a hot commodity in 1984. It was important to find a label that was receptive to that opportunity.

In an interview with *Thrasher* magazine, Hetfield commented on the trend: "Right then there were bands being signed, snatched up on major labels. All the major labels were saying, 'Oh, metal's like this new thing, get in on the money right now.'" Although the band received some criticism for signing with a big label, it didn't bother them. It was merely be the start of many accusations of selling out.

Elektra reissued *Ride the Lightning* soon after taking the band on and released a lavish 12" single. At the core of the single was "Creeping Death," and the B-side included two covers: Diamond Head's "Am I Evil?" and Blitzkrieg's "Blitzkrieg." Both versions turned out incredibly well and were regularly aired as part of the live set.

Following the reissue and the EP, *Ride the Lightning* caught on, despite very little radio play. The band toured extensively, first through Europe beginning in November and then through the US after a festive break in San Francisco.

During that break, Metallica's housemates in London, Exciter, were due to play a show in Berkeley. As Dan Beehler explained, things didn't go according to plan: "We canceled the gig because the lights didn't show up, and I'll never forget James standing in the street saying 'Hey, man, you gotta play, man!' And we said, 'No, we're leaving.' To which James replied, 'Nobody else gives a shit. Why don't you guys just play the fuckin' gig?'"

Beehler found Hetfield's reaction amusing. He recalled, "I remember him standing there beside our van in the street. He's looking at me shaking his head, saying, 'We play with no lights, why the fuck can't you?'"

On the American leg of the tour, Metallica coheadlined the first half with WASP and headlined the second part on their own, with Armored Saint as support. Anyone who witnessed that tour, which amusingly was called Bang the Head That Doesn't Bang, was stunned at how far the band had come since they had last been out on the road.

When that tour rolled through Texas, James met another aspiring group of musicians who were trying to establish their own metal immortality. That band was called Pantera, and their bass player, Rex Brown, recalled meeting up: "We had seen them on the Raven tour in a tiny place and nobody was there, but we never got to meet them."

At that time, Pantera were a glam-influenced band with a distinctly Southern flavor, and their ace card was the inhuman guitar skill of Darrell "Dimebag" Abbott. Brown recalled, "We were playing clubs in the Southwest at that time, and [singer] Philip [Anselmo] wasn't even in our band by this time. Anyhow, Dime and me go on stage with James and the guys and we go through several songs from their first record."

Even at that time, Hetfield had a considerable aura of respect, according to Brown. He said, "We looked up to him so much, we just kind of let him talk. He . . . definitely had a mystique. He had something going on upstairs, but you didn't really know what the fuck it was." A friendship was cemented, and the careers of Pantera and Metallica had considerable interplay over the next fifteen years.

David Ellefson also caught Metallica on that tour, and he noticed a change, particularly in Hetfield: "They came through and played the Palladium in Hollywood on the Ride the Lightning tour, and holy smokes, they were ferocious." It wasn't just how they sounded. Ellefson recalled, "It's impregnated on my mind watching James come out. He had his shirt off, looked great and was just ferocious. He came out roaring with confidence and was like a lion up there. He commanded the entire room. I was just floored at how great he'd become."

Another character that eased into Metallica's world was a young guy from Arizona named Eric Braverman. He was a young metal-head trying to make his way in metal journalism with his friend Joe Lopez.

Braverman recalled meeting Hetfield and Burton on that tour: "We went down—and in those days you could just call a publicist, and they'd set you up . . . and saw the band on that tour. I met them after that show and had a smoke with Cliff Burton, the only one who wanted a smoke." Braverman operated on the fringes of the band thereafter, initially as a fan, but he would later play a vital role.

Brian Slagel hung out with James after shows on that tour. He noticed a difference in Hetfield's onstage proficiency but saw little change in James on a personal level: "We'd go out after a show and hang out quite a lot actually, but for me they hadn't changed at all. Especially James."

By the time the tour ended, Metallica had rammed their music down the throats of American metal fans. While undoubtedly exhausting, the tour was a huge commercial success. The band needed time off, so part of 1985 was spent back in San Francisco relaxing, with some thought given to their next album, for which recording was scheduled to begin in September.

Katon De Pena's band, Hirax, played a gig in San Francisco while Metallica were off the road, which James attended. "I remember Metallica was getting really popular and people were starting to get jealous of them," De Pena recalled. "James and I were outside a club and were walking to a liquor store when this metal dude yells at him: 'Hey, Metallica suck!' I'll never forget the cool way James handled this dick. He didn't get mad. He just turned round and said two words: 'Your mother!' This guy had no answer because James had made him look completely stupid with just two words. I really admired that."

Before recording for the next album started, Metallica traveled to Europe for the Monsters of Rock festival in England. Awful scheduling resulted in Metallica appearing between hair metal bands Bon Jovi and Ratt. As the band took the stage, James announced to the 70,000 strong crowd: "If you came here to see spandex, eye makeup and the words 'Oh, baby' in every fuckin' song, this ain't the fuckin' band!"

Metallica appeared at the Day on the Green festival in Oakland, California, a couple of weeks later. The show was one of the highlights of Metallica's career, playing in front of a staggering 90,000 screaming metalheads. Hetfield's friend, Fred Cotton, was one of them, and Hetfield's performance that day left a mark on him. Cotton recalled, "It was incredible, man, with that hometown crowd, and they just fucking blew the whole place away. I would have hated to have to set up and play after them that day."

Hetfield got in hot water for trashing the dressing room, as he told *Playboy* years later: "A buddy and I, completely ripped on Jagermeister, got it into our heads that the deli tray and the fruit had to go through a little vent. 'The vent is not big enough. Let's make a hole!' The trailer was ruined. Bill Graham—RIP—was the promoter. I was summoned to his office."

This kind of behavior did not go down well, and Hetfield at least considered changing his ways: "I realized at that point that there was more to being in a band than pissing people off and smashing things up."

This was the end of a hugely productive chapter in the band's career. With only one more live appearance before Metallica reentered the studio, at the Lorely Metal Hammer Fest in Germany on September 14, it was also a period that offered little respite from hard work. Fortunately, both individually and collectively, they were up to the challenge. Ulrich had already begun the laborious task of tracking drums for the new record.

CHAPTER 7
THE MASTER

Although by the autumn of 1985 Metallica were making big waves in their world, their impact on the global mainstream music market was still insignificant. To hope that a metal band—and an extreme one at that—was about to gatecrash the upper reaches of the *Billboard* charts was a forlorn notion in the cautiously conservative mid-1980s.

Thrash metal was a movement within a movement, and it would be some years before a band like Metallica would be heard by "regular" people. Any such infiltration by supposedly heavier artists was far more likely for Ozzy Osbourne, Bon Jovi or Van Halen, who were working on big albums and had an image and a sound that were much easier for the public to stomach. That said, there was important Metallica business to be done, and the band took their music commitments very seriously, with a focus on detail bordering on the compulsive.

Metallica had to decide where their third album would be recorded. Contrary to popular opinion, Metallica had—at least in principle—considered other options other than *Ride the Lightning*'s producer Flemming Rasmussen. It was even rumored that Martin Birch, producer of some of Iron Maiden's best albums, was mentioned.

Nobody argued with the first-class job Rasmussen had done, particularly given his rapidly closing time window. But there was a feeling that Hetfield wanted to record in the US, and Rasmussen wasn't thrilled about traveling there to do it. What settled the matter was Ulrich's urge to work in Copenhagen, which made the choice of Rasmussen even more appealing.

The band arrived at Sweet Silence in September 1985. Hetfield and Ulrich had spent time earlier that year working on ideas for the new album. Unlike during the *Ride the Lightning* sessions, when the band crashed in the studio and Lars's friends' apartments, the band could now afford to stay in a hotel. Rasmussen recalled that they didn't use it much: "We worked nights generally; starting at 8:00 pm and working through until the morning. Then the band would go back to their hotel, pig out on the breakfast buffet and go to bed."

The hotel accommodation was necessary. In contrast to their two previous studio stints—which had lasted two weeks and one month, respectively—the three grueling months it took to record the third album was unprecedented. It took longer because of the perfectionism that Hetfield and Ulrich had honed as their career picked up steam.

Not only did they record with a manic attention to detail, they also extended that discipline to mixing and mastering. The new songs were more complex, which stretched out every part of the process. They did arrive fully prepared, as Rasmussen acknowledged with some relief: "The songs were almost all arranged when they came to the studio, as they have always been renowned for doing really good demos, and that was the case this time too." Although the album would be mixed in the US at Amigo Studios in North Hollywood by Michael Wagener, the bulk of the recording was done in these three months in Denmark.

Rasmussen recognized the change in Hetfield immediately: "When we came into the studio this time he'd improved significantly. He'd gained a lot of experience from being on the road, and as a guitar player he'd become fast and extremely accurate. When we did *Ride the Lightning* I thought he was one of the best guitar players I'd ever worked with. Now he was light-years ahead of anything I'd ever heard before."

Rasmussen thought that Hetfield had grown up rather quickly: "James is one of the most stand-up guys ever. There are tons of layers below the persona he projects, but he makes a pretty good job of hiding that—at least he certainly did in those days. It's probably part of the process of growing up that you realize you don't have to be embarrassed about emotions and stuff."

That appraisal of the Hetfield's psyche in 1985 was astute, and how much he'd developed as a guitar player became increasingly evident. Hetfield was evolving as a musician and a man, and the evidence was deeply ingrained in the new album, *Master of Puppets*.

Mention that name to any metal fan, and the praise might never stop. Ask a few non-metal types if they've heard of it and you might get the odd nod of vague recognition. *Master of Puppets*, despite its rightful place alongside Slayer's astonishing *Reign in Blood* as one of the two best thrash metal albums of all time, was still a thrash metal album. It was a phenomenal record, but it didn't cross over into the mainstream.

Master of Puppets heralded the dawning of a new type of powerful metal: metal with crushing brutality as expected by extreme fans, but also with texture, complexity and lyrical depth. It attracted a slew of new fans. It's truly a one-off, and for many it was the finest hour for Hetfield and Co.

The overall sound of the album warrants close examination. Despite being recorded in the same studio as *Ride the Lightning*, the two albums sound nothing like each other. The former has an aura of airy approachability, whereas the latter sounds distant and a little claustrophobic—a feel that perfectly suits the songs' repressive subject matter. According to Rasmussen, everyone was more dedicated to making a great-sounding record: "On *Ride the Lightning* we'd been meticulous as to how we did things. This time it was bordering on the obsessional. I think we all, including me, felt that we had an epic album. James and I were very keen to thicken everything up considerably on *Master of Puppets*. Up until then he didn't have much experience of guitar dubbing effects, and we used way more of those this time." The resulting sound is much bigger, and those multilayered guitar tracks Rasmussen mentioned give the songs an incredibly strong sound.

It wasn't just Hetfield's guitar parts that underwent an overhaul. Whereas Ulrich's drum sound on *Ride the Lightning* has a lot of reverb, giving it a rather relaxed feel, on *Master of Puppets*, it is as if every atom of air had been sucked from the studio when he laid down his drum tracks. It really is that dry and direct.

Combine all that with a level of songwriting complexity (three tracks exceed the eight-minute mark) that was a step ahead of anything they'd done previously, and you have an album whose sound and composition will never feel dated. Although *Master of Puppets* is a significant advancement, it is not as big a progression as had occurred from *Kill 'Em All* to *Ride the Lightning.*

"Battery" opens the record in understated fashion. Then, in a manner so measured but so terrifyingly powerful, that lilting acoustic part is repeated, this time by a salvo that sounds like a thousand guitars—given Hetfield's fondness for tracking, that could have been the case. Rasmussen delivered the facts, however: "It was eight rhythm guitar tracks on there."

Truly, it's a stunning moment, and one that Hetfield and Co. would never match for sheer dramatic effect. What follows is a pulverizing riff from Hetfield, whose direction and form are difficult to pin down. Then Hetfield's vocals arrive, and they are deeper, more mature and far more menacing than at any time previously. Gone are the screams, the occasional off-key notes and the weird pronunciation.

The title track that follows almost without pause is a vast, twisting arrangement and a stark antidrug warning. It is as complex and well crafted a composition as the band had ever attempted. The melancholy midsection offsets the power of the main verse and chorus superbly. Hetfield's lyrics are thoughtful and cautionary.

Reminiscent of the quiet buildup from "Fade to Black" on *Ride the Lightning*, "Welcome Home (Sanitarium)" is another example of how far the band had come. A clean intro (which starts in mono before switching over to stereo) decorated with some sublime Hammett soloing slides into another suffocating lyric by Hetfield. The lyrics portray the feelings of somebody incarcerated in a mental institution. That person's frustration builds along with the tempo of the track, culminating in a violent, angry conclusion.

Continuing a pattern Metallica had started on *Ride the Lightning*, *Master of Puppets* has an instrumental track: a gem called "Orion." Beginning with a crunchy, composed riff before branching off into some clever interplay between Hetfield and Hammett, the latter part of the tune is all Burton, with a stunning bass solo.

The album is brought to a breathless conclusion with unadulterated thrash metal. "Damage, Inc." fades in with a terrifying malevolence, an effect created by Rasmussen by reversing some prerecorded bass sounds. "Damage, Inc." is a brutal trip through a Hetfield lyrical composition that focuses on an explosive release of aggression.

In January 1986, *Master of Puppets* was sent to Wagener for mixing at his studio in Hollywood. Wagener, a gifted producer, saw two sides to the young Hetfield at the time: "James was young and wild, of course, but he still had an impressive calm when it came to understanding the direction of the album." It appeared that Hetfield had a fixed plan as to how the record should sound, even after three punishing months recording in Denmark. Wagener recalled, "He and Lars attended every single mixing session, and James had very definite needs. Those needs combined with my personal vision are what you hear on the album."

The cover art for the album is a compelling image, featuring rows of white gravestones that look like a military cemetery. A pair of large, godlike hands seemingly influence events from high above.

The band split up prior to the album's release. While Ulrich roamed Europe telling anyone who'd listen how good the record was, Hetfield was back in the Bay Area taking it easy. He hung around with friends like Fred Cotton, whom he hadn't seen much of lately.

Cotton and two other buddies had formed a joke band playing awful cover tunes. He recalled, "We got ourselves on a bill at some nightclub, and our aim was to be as shitty as possible. We wanted to see how long it was before they kicked us offstage." That band became known as Spastik Children. It was only a matter of time before Hetfield joined the fun, as Cotton confirmed: "We'd already played once by the time James came back from recording, and I told him all about it. And he said, 'Fuck, I wanna play drums.'"

According to Cotton, the point was not the music. It was about being shitty, and Hetfield relished his temporary role as the band's drummer. From all reliable reports, he could play, as Cotton testified: "Oh, yeah, he was a pounder. He liked to smash on the right cymbal . . . it was all about just having a lot of fun."

Cotton was a valuable friend in those days, and apparently Spastik Children was calming for James, away from the serious business of Metallica. "We were like fuckin' brothers back then. I taught him to ride a motorcycle and we used to skateboard together too," Cotton recalled. "James would always get ahead of himself, though, which is how he ended up breaking things." Cotton's mention of motorcycles is significant. While James probably didn't have the time or the financial means to pursue this interest then, in later life he accrued a collection of bikes, trucks and old Chevrolet cars from the year of his birth.

When Lars returned from hawking *Master of Puppets* around Europe, he and James took a vacation together in the Bahamas, while Q Prime looked for the best tour options. What they came up with was a masterstroke, as the band would tour the US extensively with Ozzy Osbourne.

After parting ways with Black Sabbath in 1979, Osbourne achieved considerable success with his own band, greatly helped by the guitar virtuosity of Randy Rhoads. Just as things were starting to roll for them, on a day off in 1982, Rhoads was killed when a light aircraft that was buzzing by the band's tour bus crashed and exploded into flames. The following year Osbourne recruited former Ratt and Rough Cutt guitarist Jake E. Lee to fill Rhoads's large shoes.

That lineup released the well-received *Bark at the Moon* in 1983 and was working on *The Ultimate Sin,* which was released the day after *Master of Puppets* on February 22, 1986. Although the two bands were worlds apart in sound, Ozzy was on a commercial high and was a significant draw, so any exposure Metallica got on such a high-profile tour could only be a positive.

Following the release of *Master of Puppets* on February 21, and thanks to Lars's efforts in Europe and a thorough media campaign by Music for Nations, sales were phenomenal. Thrash metal was gaining an unprecedented level of respectability. In both Europe and the US, a number of acts with serious thrash pretensions appeared, although none of them—with the possible exception of Slayer—had captured the public's attention quite like Metallica had.

Slayer, while regarded as one of the big four of thrash bands, was not similar to Metallica in ideology or in sound. They relied on an unmistakably evil menace. Although it gradually became more refined over the years, Slayer's music was far less progressive—and less commercially viable—than Metallica's.

With an emerging undercurrent of support, Metallica embarked on the three-month tour with Osbourne beginning on March 27. It was a challenge to see if they could turn the ear of Osbourne's more mainstream following. They needn't have worried because the gigs were a rousing success, and Metallica's harder-edged riffs were lapped up by all who saw them. More dates were added later in the summer as well as a European tour in the fall.

What they hadn't bargained on was what happened on July 26 before a show in Evansville, Indiana. Hetfield was skateboarding before the show, and as Cotton alluded to earlier, he perhaps got ahead of himself and broke his wrist. That night's show had to be canceled, but there was a bigger problem. Hetfield wouldn't be able to play guitar because of his plastered arm until late September. John Marshall, Hammett's roadie, played Hetfield's rhythm parts from the wings for the remaining Ozzy dates and part of the upcoming European jaunt with Anthrax.

When asked how hard it was to dial in Hetfield's otherworldly rhythm parts, Marshall was honest when speaking to writer Joel McIver: "Well, the hard part was trying to match the vibe and intensity of his guitar playing. I knew how to play the riffs and song arrangements okay, but getting the feel right was difficult." Marshall revealed his fear: "I think I was more worried about what the rest of the band thought than what the audience thought."

It didn't matter what the band thought, because they were lucky to have a stand-in, let alone one who was already in a band. (Marshall was a member of Metal Church.) That level of experience helped Marshall deliver something close to Hetfield levels of precision. "I remember feeling really excited, a little stunned that they had actually asked me, and a little nervous," Marshall recalled.

In mid-September, Metallica flew to Europe to play ten shows with Anthrax in the UK, prior to heading over to mainland Europe to continue the Damage, Inc. Tour on their own. That UK tour with Anthrax was a massive turning point for thrash metal in Britain given the frenetic audiences that greeted these shows.

Anthrax had their own agenda. Their *Among the Living* record was due to be released the following March, representing their career's high-water mark. Anthrax drummer Charlie Benante recalled how James was during that UK tour: "At that point we were on a real good friendly basis, and after the shows we would just hang out and talk about whatever." The two bands had a lot in common from their early days in the Music Building in New York, but there was a suspicion that they were heading in different directions, which sometimes made hanging out tricky.

After laying waste to ten theater-size venues in the UK with Anthrax, Metallica took a ferry to Sweden to continue their European tour. By this time Hetfield's wrist was almost healed, and he was keen to get back on guitar—which he did at Stockholm's Solnhallen. Later that night, the Metallica convoy of two buses left for Copenhagen, which involved a trip through the Swedish countryside. What happened the following morning changed Metallica forever.

The bus carrying the band swerved off the road between the towns of Ljungby and Varnamo in Sweden. Some parties reported ice on the road, but whatever the cause, Metallica's tour bus lay on its side. Obviously a large tour bus full of people and gear fell hard when it landed on its side. What was not immediately obvious to Hetfield, Ulrich, Hammett and the others who'd crawled out was that bass player

Burton was still trapped under the bus. Burton's bunk was adjacent to a window, and the crash had thrown him out of that opening.

The first response from Hetfield was anger, as he said in a 1993 interview: "I saw the bus lying right on him. I saw his legs sticking out. I freaked . . . Cliff wasn't alive anymore." Still in his underwear, Hetfield paced up and down the section of road where the bus had skidded, looking for the patch of ice that supposedly caused the incident. He later stated that he found none. The driver was subsequently determined to be not at fault for the accident, and no charges were brought against him. After all the band members and crew were taken to the hospital, the band stayed in a hotel in Llungby. Hetfield drowned his grief in copious alcohol, vented his rage and frustration by smashing hotel room windows while screaming about his friend's death.

The remainder of the European tour was canceled. Cotton was in touch with Hetfield by mail during that European trip. "James wrote me loads of letters from that time on the road, telling me what was happening. I even remember one letter where he actually said he was concerned about the tour bus," Cotton recalled. "I kept all those letters, you know, but when I moved houses I lost them all." While Cotton was primarily James's friend, he had become a good friend of Burton's, and rated him highly as a player.

Not only was Burton a gifted musician who had impacted Metallica's direction profoundly, he was also a likeable and good-hearted twenty-four-year-old man of whom Hetfield was extremely fond. Burton was not just laid-back in style, he was also a thinker.

Joel McIver, author of two related books (one of which focuses on Burton), recognized Burton's significance in Hetfeld's life, despite the two having little in common on paper. "Cliff was a punk-loving hippie from a rural SF suburb, while James was a stadium-rock–obsessed boozer from the mean streets of LA. The interesting part of their relationship was that Cliff was older and wiser and knew more about music theory."

At times, it must have seemed to James Hetfield that all the people close to him were either taken away or left of their own accord. This lack of control likely added to his desire to control events around him, as we've already acknowledged. In an interview many years later during the band's notorious *Some Kind of Monster* documentary, Hetfield summed up that feeling rather well: "The way I learned how to love things was just to choke 'em to death. You know, 'Don't go anywhere,' 'Don't leave' . . . you know, and 'You have to stay here.'"

That honest admission of how he dealt with relationships is consistent with his behavior. While it might have seemed controlling—particularly for those on the receiving end—it's impossible not to feel some sympathy for a guy who, by age twenty-three, knew more than most about loss.

Returning to San Francisco, Metallica were devastated by what had happened in Sweden. They thought that the best thing to do would be to get back out on the road. They felt that Burton would have wanted them to continue, as Hetfield suggested in an MTV interview in 1990: "The last thing Cliff would've wanted us to do was quit. He'd be the first one to kick us in the ass and make us wake up." So wake up they did, and after what they called "a brief yet intense mourning period," Metallica set about finding a bass player to replace the irreplaceable Burton.

CHAPTER 8
JASON, JAYMZ AND ERIC

"I really think that Cliff's passing affected James a great deal," Pantera's Rex Brown reckoned. Whoever replaced Burton would not have an easy time for two reasons. First, Burton was a complete one-off, and his style and attitude were crucial to the band's music between 1983 and 1986. Second, and more importantly, the remaining band members—particularly James Hetfield—were hit hard by Burton's death and had little time to grieve. To go out on the road so quickly was brave, but there was a risk they were merely papering over the emotional cracks.

The band used Brian Slagel as a sounding board for hiring a new bass player, and he thought that Joey Vera—from Armored Saint—was the most logical choice. The band already knew him well. At that point in Armored Saint's trajectory, it was a tough decision for Vera, as Slagel explained: "Joey had grown up with all those guys in that band; they were like his brothers." While Vera was flattered by Metallica's interest, he wanted to see where Armored Saint would take him and politely declined.

Eric Braverman had been in and around Tucson, Arizona, trying to get his metal magazine published when he got a phone call from his friend Joe Lopez telling him to check out a band called Flotsam and Jetsam.

Braverman went to interview the band for his new magazine. He recalled, "So I walk in there, and here's this guy called Jason Newsted with glasses on, and [he] has this little notebook, trying to be the most professional person he could ever be—because this was his first-ever interview." Bear in mind that Braverman had yet to publish an issue.

The two of them hit it off well, as Braverman recalled: "We just started talking a lot and Jason says, 'You're a funny guy, you've got a lot of information. How would you like to help me with my band and write songs with me?'" Braverman added, "I ended up writing songs for him that ended up on *No Place for Disgrace*—Flotsam and Jetsam's first major label album."

In September 1986, Braverman got a phone call from Newsted saying, "Dude, someone just called me and said Cliff Burton just died." Shocked by the tragic news about the guy he'd enjoyed a smoke with on the *Ride the Lightning* tour, Braverman called Jason back after a couple of days and said, "This is your job."

Braverman had seen Metallica on that summer's tour with Osbourne, written down the band's set list and put those songs on a tape. He recalled, "I gave Jason that tape and told his girlfriend to look after him and make sure he could sit in a room all alone and learn these songs." Newsted listened and learned the songs. Meanwhile, Braverman had already sown the Newsted seed with label boss Michael Alago and helped Newsted fly up to an audition that Alago set up.

Not only were the band immediately impressed by Newsted's playing, but they also liked his drive and passion. Newsted was first and foremost a Metallica fan, so he knew how much it meant to be on the brink of joining his favorite band. After a night of drinking at a bar in San Francisco as some kind of initiation, Newsted officially became Metallica's new bass player. Understandably the news didn't go over well with his former bandmates in Flotsam and Jetsam, although in hindsight, they must have understood. Although Flotsam and Jetsam's debut album was well received, they never enjoyed the same commercial success as Metallica.

Newsted wouldn't have a lot of time to dwell on his new position, because Metallica wanted him to play his first gig with them once he'd rehearsed all the songs to everyone's satisfaction. Braverman got dragged along that night too. He recalled, "It was an unannounced show at the Country Club in Reseda, supporting Metal Church. Jason wanted me to come out and hang out with him and do what I do."

Hetfield didn't appreciate Braverman's presence, as he recalled: "That night at the Country Club James was saying to Jason, 'Oh, so you're already bringing some Flotsam personnel along with you?' and stuff like that, and this is day one. And they were riding him [Jason] about the T-shirt he was wearing. And that kind of thing never stopped."

Newsted questioned why James was treating him like that. Braverman asked Newsted to "imagine what it'd be like if you ever disagreed with him. I told him that a hundred times." Sometime down the line, that day would come.

Interpersonal politics aside, Newsted performed that night—and at another secret gig the next night in Anaheim—as if his life depended on it. Braverman understood why: "He performed in the spirit of knowing how lucky he was. He put in twice the energy that they did. It might sound a bit corny, but he wanted to honor Cliff and his fans and family by playing an awesome show every time he went onstage."

What is worth a little examination is the early relationship between Braverman and Hetfield, because it reveals a lot about Hetfield's personality. Braverman explained, "From the very beginning, I saw a lot of him because I was with Jason. It was always like it was all a bit of a fun challenge. For example, if I was walking down the hall, he'd knock my hat off."

That was the kind of prank that Hetfield enjoyed, and given that Braverman wasn't averse to goofing around, it seemed the two had a fair bit in common. "James always liked to challenge me with snide comments and just ridiculous attitude. I actually thought that this guy was becoming a pretty good friend of mine," recalled Braverman.

Braverman had made himself a fixture at Metallica events and had also worked his way onto the writing staff of the Metallica fanzine, *So What.* "I was given pretty much *carte-blanche* to do whatever the hell I wanted for a few years. Also, in my first *Loud* magazine back in 1985, which had nonheavy bands like Keel and Bon Jovi in it, I put James Hetfield—who looks like he's fifteen—on the cover."

Braverman was keen to put forward fun ideas for the band in the fanzine, and that brought him closer to James. Braverman said, "I always just saw him as this crazy guy who'd got put in this situation, we had a good rapport and when we were interfacing we'd challenge each other because we were enjoying each other's sense of humor, and our mutual fun of [humorously] intimidating people."

The relationship was a strange one—and one that Hetfield kept at arm's length, as Braverman confirmed: "I'd always hang out with him because I was with Jason, but it never got to the stage where I could call him or something."

With little chance to get to know his bandmates and settle in, Newsted and Metallica headed out for a brief tour of Japan. The tour was a success in that it introduced Newsted to the band's audience, but in an understated way. It was also a trying time for Newsted given that Ulrich and particularly Hetfield subjected him to a series of grim initiation ceremonies, all designed to test the new guy's endurance. Hetfield and Ulrich didn't bargain on Newsted's durability, nor did they figure that their target even understood the psychology behind what they were doing.

What Newsted understood perfectly—which made Hetfield and Ulrich's actions less hurtful—was that it wasn't personal. Perhaps all Newsted represented was a "somebody" in a place that was formerly occupied by Burton. He became the most accessible target for their grief and frustration.

Hetfield, Ulrich and Hammett buried their grief and emotion under a fire blanket called Metallica. Periodically flames came out from underneath, only to be quickly extinguished. Newsted was an excellent musician and an intelligent, thoughtful man, but most of all he was a fighter. That was the quality he had to rely on most during his first five years in the band.

After the quick stint in Japan, Metallica toured the East Coast and Canada before finishing up in San Francisco on January 2, 1987. The band then went back to Europe to compensate for the shows they had canceled after the bus crash. They went back to the Netherlands to play at the Aardshock festival alongside Celtic Frost. Metallica did have further live commitments, but they weren't until the summer and in the meantime they worked on their first video.

For a band who were the antithesis of the average MTV act, it would have been surprising if they'd come up with a polished, heavily edited feature. *Cliff 'Em All*, as it was called, was anything but. It was grimy and unedited, featuring moments from Burton's era in the band that were filmed with a handheld camera.

Most of the footage was fans' material, and the rest was from the band and crew. Hetfield wrote some notes of his own on the cover, and the whole thing had the feel of a bootleg, which was intentional. Hetfield's notes were amusing to say the least, summed up by the words "The quality in some places ain't that happening, but the feeling is there and that's what matters!!!" He then signed off as "Jaymz," a pen name he'd use for many years in fanzines and other written messages to the fans.

It looked like this was Hetfield's disclaimer for the video. But his words were a touching public tribute to Cliff. It gave clues that there was a sensitive side in there, and that in the right—or the wrong—circumstances, it would come to the surface. Fans 'got' it, and *Cliff 'Em All* was a worthy addition to any fan's collection.

That spring, the band was in San Francisco. Hetfield was back with Cotton, taking it easy before summer festival appearances. Ulrich and Newsted fixed up a garage in a house Ulrich had just bought, with the goal of turning it into a private rehearsal space.

John Kornarens, who was still a good friend, came up and helped with DIY work to make the place useable. "Jason was pretty good at that stuff, and when James was around he was okay too," Kornarens recalled.

You would think that moving stuff around in a garage and using power tools would present more danger than hanging out and having fun would. It was Hetfield who presented the band with their next problem, one that was becoming rather familiar. Hetfield, Cotton, Hammett and a couple of others had gone to Oakland Hills to hang out and skateboard. Cotton recalled: "We were at this empty swimming pool at this old abandoned hotel and we were skating again. James got up a little too high as usual!"

When Hetfield came down, things weren't good. Cotton recalled, "I heard his arm snap and James shouted, 'Oh fuck! It's broke!' I had to take him to Highland Hospital in Oakland, which is just a county hospital and is in a tough neighborhood, but it was the closest one."

Cotton said, "We went in and he was all right, but he had a compound fracture and his bone had popped out of his arm. The nurse came out and said, 'He wants you in here with him,' and I was teasing him because they had him hooked up to IVs and shit."

"He screamed out in pain and the nurse had to take this long Q-tip to make sure that it was the bone that had made the cut, so she stuck it all the way in his arm," Cotton said. After that they gave him some drugs and did surgery to fix the break, and very soon James was fooling around. Cotton recalled: "He was fine and recovering, flicking boogers at the wall and shit."

The several weeks it would take for Hetfield's arm to heal meant that the band couldn't do any serious rehearsal of new material as planned. Instead they did an EP of cover versions as a stopgap project. Most of the tracks were by bands that had influenced or inspired Metallica, and the production sounds like they were playing in *your* living room more so than theirs—which was the desired effect. It really was that live and energetic, and you can hear Hetfield's fingers grating on the strings as he chiseled out some awesome riffs.

The first selection was "Helpless" by NWOBHM pioneers (and Lars's friends) Diamond Head. To say it's impressive would be an understatement. The original version is a great song—but Hetfield's precision riffing is as astounding as it'd ever been, and the monstrous rhythm section of Ulrich and Jason "Newkid" Newsted, as he'd been dubbed, is equally compelling.

Next is "The Small Hours" by British band Holocaust, and on this track, velocity is replaced by sheer heaviness. Killing Joke's "The Wait" follows, and Newsted's rumbling bass precedes "Crash Course in Brain Surgery," originally performed by Budgie.

The final song is a medley of two tunes by punk band The Misfits, "Last Caress" and "Green Hell." Apparently it was Burton who'd alerted Hetfield to The Misfits' aggressive style and horror movie imagery. The manner in which these two punk tracks were tackled—particularly by Hetfield—is indicative of the band's versatility as well as the thin line that exists between thrash metal and punk as genres.

The EP carries the title *The $5.98 EP* and the subtitle *Garage Days Revisited*. It was recorded quickly—at least by Metallica's standards—at A&M and Conway studios in LA (after Ted Nugent was persuaded to vacate the place for the six days that Metallica needed).

It hit the shops on August 21, 1987, to rave reviews. The sleeve, like the *Cliff 'Em All* video, features a scrawled note to fans, explaining the laidback ideology behind this excellent EP.

The band returned to England that month for the Monsters of Rock Festival, and to warm up they played a secret gig at London's 100 Club, under the not-so-secret sobriquet "Damage, Inc."

There were more Metallica fans in London who saw through the name than there was space for them in this intimate venue. Less intimate was the vast throng that turned up at the festival to see Metallica alongside Bon Jovi, who were flying high on the heavy-selling *Slippery When Wet*—a commercial album of pomp-rock anthems that was mixed by a Canadian sound engineer and producer named Bob Rock.

Despite the obvious stylistic differences between the two main bands, the festival was a success, if for no other reason than that it helped promote Metallica's recent EP. One more festival appearance in Nuremberg, supporting classic rock gods Deep Purple, ended Metallica's commitments for the year. The four band members dispersed to start giving thought to material for Metallica's fourth album.

CHAPTER 9
DORIS

James Hetfield and Metallica had a considerable chunk of time off in the latter part of 1987. The band went their separate ways to relax and live life, prior to regrouping to plan their next move. "This was the only time we'd really get to see James and the guys. They had become such road dogs; they were hardly ever in town," Ron Quintana recalled.

During this hiatus, each member worked on their own ideas with riff tapes, which they later contributed towards the next album. Each player—who probably had some kind of home recording space—would commit any ideas, riffs or fully formed songs onto tape, so that they could listen to them later and keep the good stuff for the record. The remainder would be stored away for future use or perhaps discarded. Historically, mainly Hetfield's and Ulrich's material made the cut, but on occasion some contributions from others would sneak in. Newsted was a keen composer of new material, and he kept busy doing just that, while occasionally hanging out with his buddy Eric Braverman.

James lived with his girlfriend, Teresa, during these fall months—in an apartment in Talbot Street in El Cerrito. In his free time he hung out with Fred Cotton as well as Jim and Lou Martin.

Jim Martin was a friend of Burton and a member of the Spastik Children project that both Hetfield and Burton had endorsed. He played guitar in alternative metal giants Faith No More before leaving the band in 1993. James liked to hang out with the Martins, drink beer and mess around.

Eric Braverman remembered running into James and the Martin brothers—an anecdote that he wrote about in *So What* and recounted for the author: "Jason and I went on this trip to a place in [Northern] California. It's actually where Cliff Burton's ashes were scattered. Lou Martin had a little cabin up there, so Jason and me went up there to meet them. Anyway, we get up there and James, Lou and Jim had been drinking a lot, so we end up having this crazy time."

Braverman escaped the mayhem for a while by going for a hike up a hill in front of the cabin, which turned out not to be a good idea. He recalled, "These guys are shooting guns everywhere and James all of a sudden says, 'Hey, take these exploding targets to the top of that hill if you're going to hike up there."

Exploding targets are little discs with orange dots on them, and when you shoot them, they blow up. Braverman continued, "So I'm up at the top of this hill and James is down at the cabin making shooting noises from this porch as if they're shooting at me. James was saying things like, 'I almost got him!' and 'I can see him there on the ridge!' to make me think they were really shooting at me, but they were shooting in the other direction!"

When Braverman returned to the cabin, James and his friends continued drinking and wanted Braverman to join in. "They were drunk and wanted me to drink this terrible port wine they had. I kept saying 'I'm not drinking it!' So all night James and Jim sang this song that went 'Eric Braverman! Drink the wine! Or you're going to walk to the airport.'"

Braverman saw the funny side of Hetfield's cabin antics—as he did with most things—and wrote about the escapade for *So What*. What he didn't bargain on was the backlash that Hetfield would receive from irate parents of Metallica fans. Braverman explained, "Soon James is getting all these letters from organizations and moms and dads about gun safety, and drinking with guns, etc."

Hetfield wrote a rebuttal, which appeared in his own handwriting in the next issue of *So What*. He pointed out that all his guns were legally acquired, he had trained extensively and the firearms were kept under the required lock and key. He pointed out that people had different opinions about all manner of things, and guns were one such area—but that the world was "huge" and people were entitled to their own hobbies. He asked that readers take Braverman's article "with a block of salt [the word 'grain' was crossed out], it's a story that has been exaggerated . . . and really, really, really exaggerated." He added that "the article was written for entertainment and humor."

When Hetfield saw Braverman next, he went up to him and said, "You fuckin' nut!"

As 1987 moved on, the specifics of Metallica's fourth album were high on the agenda, and one question was who should produce it. There was no problem with the job Flemming Rasmussen had done on *Master of Puppets*, and its huge success and longevity are ample testimony to that fact.

Rasmussen was committed to another project at the time (a Danish band called Danish Pregnant Woman). Metallica reluctantly looked for someone new and had a good idea who that would be.

Earlier that year, a producer named Mike Clink was involved with a monstrously successful album by LA rockers Guns N' Roses. *Appetite for Destruction* had crushed everything in its path and had several hit singles, of which "Sweet Child O' Mine" was the commercial zenith. Not only was *Appetite* a great mixture of raw, sleazy tunes, it also sounded fantastic—with a bass-led depth that gave the songs some added power.

None of this was lost on Hetfield and Ulrich, and they liked the way the album sounded, not to mention its sales. They hired Clink to produce their fourth record, *...And Justice for All*. Apparently, most of the songs were far along before the assigned date to enter the studio, January 19, 1988. The album promised to be another major leap forward.

In an interview with *Music and Sound Output* in 1988, Hetfield and Ulrich explained their processes. "We've got riffs from years and years," said Hetfield. "On the road we constantly riff and write it down." That material was then sifted through and divided into individual categories, Hetfield explained: "Like, some shit is strong enough to be the main idea of a tune. Then we go through the tapes and try to find possible bridges, choruses, middle bits or whatever. After we have a skeleton of a song, we start getting a feel for what the song is really like. Then we search for a title from a list of titles that fits with the riffing's mood." At that point, Hetfield's "songs" were almost at the demo stage and ready to record. Sessions were booked for One on One Studios in LA.

Right from the beginning there was a complication. According to Lars, it was all the ancillary distractions that went with being in a studio in LA rather than Copenhagen. "You walk in there and there's eight secretaries, computers and fuckin' fax machines. I know the stuff is necessary, but there comes a point where it's too much," he told *Music and Sound Output.*

The studio surroundings weren't the only issue, because these Clink sessions never got off the ground. Ulrich called Rasmussen and asked him to reconsider. He flew to LA two weeks later.

"The major change as far as I knew was that they'd gotten these all new Mesa Boogie amps for the guitars, and I know that there were a lot of difficulties getting the right guitar sound. And [the band] didn't really resolve that until I got there," Rasmussen recalled.

When Rasmussen arrived at One on One, he stripped down the equipment that Clink had used and started over, using some old gear that was lying around the studio. "I also had an equalizer inserted on the actual amp so that I could change the guitar sound from the control room," he added.

Further details as to why Metallica and Clink didn't hit it off are not available. But there is an irony here. Metallica backed off working with a commercially oriented producer, only to end up later with Bob Rock, one of the most commercially successful producers.

To Hetfield at least, the band couldn't work with anyone other than Rasmussen at that point. "Well, we can, but it's a slow process," Hetfield told *Music and Sound Output.* Rasmussen and Metallica recorded the record at One on One and surfaced sometime in May with a record that just needed mixing. Shortly afterward, James flew to San Francisco to visit Cotton, before Metallica went out on the Van Halen– headlined Monsters of Rock Tour.

"James came up to visit and my sister had to book him a hotel room because he didn't have any ID," Cotton recalled. Hetfield had a cassette tape with him of the recorded but unmixed *...And Justice for All.* "The one he brought me had no vocal tracks on it, and I said 'This is done?' It was as heavy as hell," Cotton said. "I was fucking blown away at how it sounded."

Cotton was lucky, because that cassette contained sounds that the wider listening public would never hear, which brings us to one of the most discussed issues in Metallica's entire career: the final mix of *...And Justice for All.*

"It had bass on it when I finished with it, that's all I know," Rasmussen confirmed. "I wasn't there when it was mixed, but the guys who mixed it were Steve Thompson and Michael Barbiero. It was a fight between Lars and James about having the guitars or the drums loudest, and during that process they kind of forgot about the bass."

Lonn Friend—who was the executive editor of *RIP* magazine, the first nonporn title published by iconic pornographer Larry Flynt—was at the box office of The Roxy on Sunset Boulevard one night in late 1987, waiting to see "some obscure band." Across the lobby he spotted two long-haired guys standing and talking.

"Hey, you're James and Lars from Metallica," Friend announced. "I introduced myself and Lars recognized my name from an article I'd written for a men's magazine about porn films in Paris. James laughed and suggested that we blow the band off and head next door to the Rainbow for a beer, which we did, and we spent the next couple of hours talking, connecting. They told me they were in Hollywood recording their album ...*And Justice for All.*"

Friend was stunned by Hetfield's modest persona at the time: "My first impression of James was: *here's a musician who keeps himself to himself and lets his music do his talking.*" While Ulrich did a lot of the talking that night, James played his part too. "James would toss in a quick-witted one-liner here and there. He was authentic, didn't give any signals he was in a rock band, far less a very successful one," Friend recalled, clearly impressed.

While giving no such indication to outsiders like Friend, egos seemingly got in the way of making the record sound good. It has been suggested that the lack of bass was a direct attempt by James to isolate and humble Newsted.

The process of recording the bass parts hadn't made Newsted feel welcome, given that he was largely on his own and got little to no input from Hetfield or Ulrich. It wasn't that the parts he had were particularly complex either. For his first full album with Metallica, his remit was to follow James's guitar parts.

You wouldn't know that from listening to the final mix, as far as Rasmussen was concerned: "James told Steve Thompson 'Make the bass so you can just hear it, and then take it three beats down.' I know there is really good bass on there because it was there when I recorded it. It's fantastic, and most of the time it just octaves the rhythm guitars. But there are some other bits in there which really should have been heard."

Pantera's Rex Brown had the definitive account of the bass issue, which put this long-running saga to bed for good. Brown explained, "They had just finished *...And Justice for All,* and we were hanging out at some club, sitting out listening to it, and there's no bass on it. They're laughing their asses off saying, 'We got this new guy Jason Newsted, and we're fucking him. We're just not going to put his bass in the mix.' We were all laughing about it."

Despite mixed messages about what happened with the mixed levels, it was seemingly a deliberate act to omit Newsted's bass parts. "They were fucking howling about it!" Brown recalled. "It was just harassment, and very intentional. I kept saying 'Where's the bass?' James just said 'Ha ha, there's none on it.'"

Whatever the circumstances, the finished product's legacy was the songs. For many fans, *...And Justice for All* was the band's most compelling listen, despite its bizarre sonic elements.

Any misgivings about the mix were dispelled by the opening track "Blackened," whose menacing intro escapes the speakers, fading in amid an ominous dual guitar wail. As that intro ends, Ulrich's drums engage—ahead of a clinically potent Hetfield riff that slows to a midtempo pace for the verse.

The intelligent lyrical content on tracks like "Blackened" was not lost on peers like Kreator's Mille Petrozza: "I love some of his lyrics on *...And Justice for All.* It's my favorite album of theirs, and James's stuff has a very smart and critical undertone."

Petrozza was correct, as the album questions the true value—and existence of—the concept of justice. The title track comes next and encapsulates the theme with a running time of almost ten minutes.

During that period it twists and turns but always sticks to the same feel. The song is a monument to the development of the band at that time. It became their progressive masterpiece, as well as the last time they'd deliver such an overtly complex track.

Anyone that thought James Hetfield had reached his lyrical high point on the band's previous album hadn't bargained for his depth and clever use of words on this album. "He is a masterful, underrated wordsmith. It's crazy! It's, like, 'How did you do that?'" Braverman said of Hetfield's lyrics.

"Eye of the Beholder" follows with a fade-in intro and a pounding, almost tribal Ulrich drum pattern.

The track that comes next, "One," is the token "quiet" (initially, at least) song. It brought about the band's first bigger-budget video. The video's footage is intercut with scenes from the 1971 antiwar film *Johnny Got His Gun*, directed by Michael Salomon—the story of a World War I victim who returns home unable to speak or move. Sonically, it is a close relative of "Fade to Black" and "Welcome Home (Sanitarium)" from the previous two albums.

"Shortest Straw" follows, and on first listen, it's hard to pin down. Over time it is one of the tracks that has endured best, a belief that Ulrich has shared. The lead single from the album is "Harvester of Sorrow"—the harrowing tale of a father who reputedly slaughters his family for no obvious reason other than his own dwindling sanity. It is arguably a strange choice for a single given its slow tempo. Fans of the band got the opportunity to hear it in advance of the album's release—given that it was performed at many of the Monsters of Rock shows—and it has always been a live favorite. "Frayed Ends of Sanity" follows and, like "Shortest Straw," has aged well.

As had become the pattern, there is one instrumental track (if you discount the few lines of Hetfield speaking). It's a remnant of Cliff Burton's riff writing, entitled, rather prophetically, "To Live Is to Die." Its lilting, cleanly picked intro builds up to a jagged, stop-start riff.

The final track on *...And Justice for All* is a gem, punctuated by the torrent of frustration Hetfield emits—seemingly about his parents. Called "Dyer's Eve," it is one of the more obvious lyrical rants about his upbringing that Hetfield ever recorded. For some, this track, more than any other in the Metallica canon, illustrates Hetfield's feelings about his childhood. It seems to have been a cathartic exercise, as he never went quite this far again.

...And Justice for All is a well-rounded, progressive metal record, with a staggering attention to detail that more than makes up for its sonic failings. To the general public it is still tarred with a broad thrash metal brush, but for devoted fans of both the band and thrash, *...And Justice for All* represents a subtle move towards the mainstream.

The sleeve features cover art by Brian "Pushead" Schroeder and depicts Lady Justice bound in chains and blindfolded. On the tour that followed, "Doris," as she would be nicknamed, was an integral part of the stage set, her crumbling form a symbol of failed justice.

Metallica had already been touring the US since May as part of the Monsters of Rock extravaganza, which featured Van Halen/Led Zeppelin–influenced Kingdom Come and Dokken.

Hetfield confirmed the party atmosphere in an interview with Metal Hammer magazine: "That was the Jagermeister days. I am still hearing stories about it, like that I slugged Lars but I don't remember any of it. We were drunk the whole time. We were very much into drinking and having a good fucking time. That was the pinnacle of all the debauchery, drinking, fucking and general insanity."

While the band were out of control on tour, Master of Puppets was certified platinum. That achievement augured well for the new record, which was going to be pushed harder as a result of wide-reaching touring.

When ...*And Justice for All* was released on September 5, 1988, the band were in a serious touring groove. This was great preparation for their own trek, called Damaged Justice, which began in Europe six days later. The critics' response to the album was largely positive: "Thrash is too demeaning a term for this metametal, a marvel of precision-channeled aggression," Rolling Stone reckoned.

Metallica toured mainland Europe, the UK and Ireland, with support from ex-Misfits member Glenn Danzig's namesake band. Queensrÿche provided support for additional gigs in Europe through November 5.

During a week-long break prior to the US leg of the tour, Hetfield was back in San Francisco briefly. He went to one of his old haunts the Stone to see Kreator play. "Someone told me James was there, and before we went onstage the band were all excited!" Petrozza recalled. "But we never got the chance to meet."

It wasn't all free time, as the band recorded the video for "One," editing it down from the eight-minute-plus version. It wasn't meant to be a standard "live" performance video, nor was it a Hollywood piece with scantily clad models pawing at the band's pelvic areas.

It is a rather depressing video, featuring footage of a hapless—and for that matter limbless—war veteran writhing on a hospital bed, while the band grimly thrashes away in what looks like a dimly lit warehouse. It is hardly your standard MTV fare, and is far from a commercial sellout.

Heading into 1989, the Damaged Justice Tour continued through the Midwest, while the album sold by the cartload. Metallica were nominated for a Grammy in February 1989, in the category of Best Heavy Metal Performance. The band were edged out by prehistoric folk-rock act Jethro Tull, who, besides not being a true heavy metal act, didn't even have an album out at the time.

Metallica's US tour ground on through March and April until Queensrÿche left the bill, but not before James had Chippendale-type dancers invade the stage during Queensrÿche's set on the last night. Metallica kicked off an Australasian tour, with support from The Cult. Shows in Hawaii, Japan and Alaska brought the tour back to Canada before swinging through the Midwest.

Producer Bob Rock caught the Damaged Justice Tour when it rolled into Vancouver. He was about to help resurrect Mötley Crüe's wobbling career by producing their career-best offering, Dr. Feelgood. Rock gave the album a beefy bass-led sound in the same way that Mike Clink had done for Appetite for Destruction, which wasn't lost on Hetfield and Ulrich when they heard that record.

Rock introduced himself to the band that night in Vancouver and was seemingly blown away by the band's live sound. He told them that they had not even come close to capturing that energy on record. That didn't sit well with Hetfield and Ulrich. At the same time, a seed of doubt was sown about the band's next direction, even though ...And Justice for All had been a resounding commercial and creative success, peaking at Number 6 on the *Billboard* chart.

On the Canadian leg of the tour, Dan Beehler of Exciter got to see James again. He recalled, "They came to my hometown of Ottawa and it was great. He's got that big smile, and they treated me awesome that night." While Metallica were a different band now, Beehler was pleasantly surprised by how little James had changed: "He hadn't changed at all. As soon as he saw me it was like the old days. I guess he has a soft spot for people from his past."

When the draining Damaged Justice Tour came to an end, Hetfield and Ulrich dropped off most people's radars until early 1990, when it was announced they would contribute a cover version of Queen's "Stone Cold Crazy" to an Elektra compilation. Apart from a February appearance at the Grammys, where Metallica picked up an award for the "One" video, very little was heard from the band for the next three months. Given the exhaustive nature of recording and touring ...*And Justice for All,* that was no great surprise.

CHAPTER 10
LIBERTY OR DEATH

To say that the early 1990s were a pivotal point for rock music would be a huge understatement. It was a fulcrum, a watershed, whatever you want to call it. Some relatively well-known bands would not survive—or would be forced to operate from a position deep underground.

The early 1990s were a critical era for Hetfield and Metallica, even though they'd reached a much larger audience with *...And Justice for All.* That was a miracle considering that it was relatively extreme music for many people's tastes. However, there was a new "scene" on the horizon. Continuing down the previous record's overtly complex and progressive path might have isolated Metallica along with similar bands as grunge was taking over American music.

Originating in Seattle, grunge was an amalgam of rock attitudes and punk rebellion, melded into a depressingly weary mixture. It spread throughout the Seattle area with early exponents like Soundgarden, Alice in Chains and Nirvana leading the way.

Jerry Cantrell was one of the founding members of Alice in Chains, and to him grunge was a retrospective label: "We were there before that word was even invented. I don't know if any of the bands were particularly comfortable with that title, but that became the catchphrase that encompassed us all. As far as I saw it, we were all just rock 'n' roll bands to some degree."

A twist of fate that helped grunge expand was the eleventh-hour inclusion of Alice in Chains on the thrash metal arena super-tour called Clash of the Titans. The tour kicked off in May 1991 and included Slayer, Megadeth and Anthrax. Alice in Chains was a late replacement for Bay Area thrash act Death Angel, which was involved in a horrific bus crash.

Although Alice in Chains stood out stylistically as part of an overtly thrash lineup—and apparently received all manner of abuse from fans—their presence promoted grunge to arena-sized audiences. Alice in Chains won some fans over, and by the time Clash of the Titans came to a halt in mid-July, grunge was on many people's radars.

Whether grunge was stylistically groundbreaking is irrelevant to this book. It was a movement that gathered a commercial following at an alarming rate, with the net result that metal—and certainly thrash metal—would soon be marginalized by this new fad. Worrying too was the fact that, while metal acts unwittingly helped their grunge colleagues by occasionally taking them out on tour, this favor was typically not returned.

While the extent of the grunge revolution was not clear until late 1991, the signs were there the preceding year. Hetfield and Ulrich were very aware of them while taking a break before recording album number five.

Metallica had never started working on an album without debating who would produce it. This time things were both more clear-cut and more controversial. It was no secret that the band recognized the work Bob Rock had done with a slew of commercial bands. You couldn't argue with his success rate.

Even James Hetfield had to grudgingly admit that he liked Rock's sound. "If you go back and look at the stuff he's produced, it sounds great, even though the songs were crap," Hetfield was quoted as saying in Chris Ingham's *Metallica: The Stories Behind the Biggest Songs.*

Hammett, a lifelong fan of The Cult, loved what Rock had done with their *Sonic Temple.* That album had made its way into the world on the back of Rock's monster production. Ulrich loved Rock's work, period.

Metallica decided that Rock would at least mix their new album. Rock wanted more. "I didn't really want to mix it," he told the *Classic Album* series. "I actually wanted to produce it," he added. The problem was that Richie Sambora—guitarist with Bon Jovi, with whom Rock had strong connections—wanted him to oversee his debut solo album, *Stranger in This Town.*

This presented Rock with an awkward dilemma. As the story goes, Rock and his family were driving through the Nevada desert on vacation and saw a guy sitting by the side of the road, in the middle of nowhere, wearing a Metallica T-shirt. This convinced him that the new Metallica album was a project he could not turn down. He told Sambora that someone else would have to produce his record.

Recording began at One on One studios in early October, with Rock overseeing proceedings. In the *Classic Albums* DVD, Rock acknowledged the band's hesitancy to move away from the regimented

way they had worked previously. This was a new working dynamic for
Hetfield in particular, given his former dominant role in the studio.
This new setup was going to test both his patience and his need to
always to be in control.

Predictably, things did not go well at the start. For the first three
months of recording, Hetfield put Rock—with assistance from his
bandmates—through a series of tests. They did the same thing to him
that they did to Newsted in 1987. Rock chose to roll with the punches,
and the band started to enjoy the process.

On previous albums each band member had recorded their parts
alone, but Rock was keen that they all play together in the studio,
giving the songs more of a live feel. By Metallica's own admission, recording had felt stiff in the past. With almost a fifth band member in
Rock, there was a more relaxed feel to recording the songs, if not the
personal relationships.

Rock let each facet of the band express itself fully, including
Newsted's bass presence. This freedom encouraged the best elements
that the band members, particularly Hetfield, had to offer flow in a
way that they never had before.

Lonn Friend, who was still working with *RIP* magazine, was invited into the secret environment of One on One studios to report on
the band's progress. "I got to examine the recording process from a very
intimate point of view during the winter of 1990 and spring of 1991,"
Lonn explained. "I brought our audience the inside story. One night
James took me into what he called his 'Tent of Doom'; that was his
tongue-in-cheek name of the area which housed the mics responsible
for picking up that classic Hetfield guitar sound."

James Hetfield performing with Obsession, his first proper band, formed in 1978.
Photo: Ron McGovney

James and Ron McGovney become faux *Hit Parader* cover stars inside a fairground photo booth, 1981.
Photo: Bill Hale

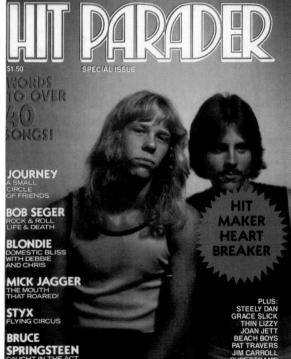

With pictures of The Scorpions and Michael Schenker on the wall, James strikes a rebellious pose, 1981.
Photo: Ron McGovney

James at Jason Newsted's house after a Flotsam and Jetsam show in San Francisco, with Mike Gilbert, Lou Martin and Brad Halverson.
Photo: Eric Braverman

Outside the Metallica Mansion on Carlson Boulevard, El Cerrito, in 1984.
Photos: "Banger" Bart

Metallica fanzine editor Steffan Chirazi, James, Kirk Hammett and Eric Braverman at Kirk's bachelor party, 1987.

James with John Marshall (Kirk Hammett's guitar tech) and others at Kirk's bachelor party.

James with tour manager Bob Schneider.

Being photographed with Jason Newsted by Ross Halfin.
Photos: Eric Braverman

James and Jim Martin, formerly of Faith No More, at Maxwell Cabin in Castro Valley, California, where Cliff Burton's ashes are scattered.

James, Jason Newsted, Lou Martin, Jim Martin and Fred Cotton at Maxwell Cabin.
Photos: Eric Braverman

James with Ron McGovney during the seemingly endless tour for "The Black Album," backstage at the LA Forum, 1992.
Photo: Ron McGovney

With Lars Ulrich and Metal Blade CEO Brian Slagel at Metal Blade's 30th anniversary party, 2012.
Photo: Stephanie Cabral

Michael Alago, who signed Metallica to the Elektra label in 1984, hangs out with his old friend backstage at Madison Square Garden, 2009.
Photo: Michael Alago

This album had the Hetfield stamp all over it, perhaps more than any record previously. "He showed me the lyrics that night, scrawlings of what would become the theme, heart and soul of that earthshaking record," Friend recalled. "There was a process to the making of that record, Lars and Bob Rock were key players, architects, holders of the script . . . but it was James and his musical genius that fed the monster as it grew." Friend recalled that, despite the pressure of delivering this monster, James remained approachable: "His personality was always humorous, rarely aloof. You could see there was a method to his madness/genius."

While Rock was the producer, Randy Staub was involved in much of the recording process. Their assistant, Mike Tacci, spoke to the author for this book. Tacci is a very intelligent and talented engineer who went on to work on records by Megadeth and Lynch Mob, among others, and he immediately recognized Hetfield's genius: "I was working with him for nine months and although I'd worked with other rock and metal bands, I was very, very impressed. James was very confident, and his musical timing was impeccable. Not just that, his lyrics were on a higher and deeper level than I'd come across, and to me he was the core of the band." Tacci added, "James was just so down-to-earth and real. He was witty, too, and a pleasure and inspiration to be around."

The album was called *Metallica*, and on account of its plain black cover, it would soon be referred to as "The Black Album."

According to Hetfield, the title and the uncluttered album cover were meant to channel the listener's attention to the music and not towards any fancy, distracting cover art—an approach that could only succeed if the songs were good. Fortunately, they were not just good;

they were, in most observers' views, astounding. From the moment *Metallica* landed on August 12, 1991, rock music would never be the same again. People lined up at record stores on the night before the release day, leading to almost 600,000 unit sales in the first week in the US alone.

The record was not so different from anything the band had done before, but it succeeded in fusing the best aspects of the past with something fresh and new. Gone were the complex and progressive sections and the ten-minute running times. They were replaced with shorter verse/chorus arrangements with big, juicy hooks.

While some die-hard fans suggested that the band had sold out, most recognized that *Metallica* was the record the band had to make. For a music industry that was approaching a crossroads, it was the right record at the right time. "It took me a while to really get it," Pantera's Rex Brown admitted. "Maybe even two years. After that I realized it was a fuckin' great record. I do think that a few kids felt shortchanged by that record at first."

The album kicks off with what would be voted by *Kerrang!* magazine's readers as The Best Metal Song of All Time: "Enter Sandman." It has all the attributes of a massive rock song with a hard edge. After that familiar haunting intro, the classic song launches into a memorable three-part circular riff that, as *Rolling Stone*'s David Fricke suggested, "blew out the speakers on the radio."

The mighty "Sad But True" follows and is, as the band's manager, Cliff Burnstein, once described it, "Music to pull teeth to." Its lazy, laid-low riff was a subject of continual discussion in the studio. Rock's suggestion to slow it down worked perfectly.

The one feature of *Metallica* that sets it apart from anything else the band had attempted is the slower songs, of which "The Unforgiven" is the first. Hetfield's harmonies are startling, and the tense lyrical content feels confessional. Old school fans initially recoiled in horror, but radio stations loved the new direction.

"Nothing Else Matters" is similarly surprising. If there was ever a track that introduced Metallica to a completely new audience, it is this heart-on-sleeve ballad. Reputedly another Hetfield confessional about missing loved ones (girlfriends specifically), it is touching. The song was a turning point in Hetfield's creative and, arguably, personal life.

In interviews, Hetfield admitted that he stumbled on the simple open-string strum by accident and that he felt uncomfortable about sharing it with the rest of the band. The song could not be omitted. Vocally, he was utterly reborn on this track. His touching harmony has a depth that nobody, perhaps even himself, thought he possessed. The blistering guitar solo that he delivered—wrought with sheer emotion—is one of his best.

Anthrax's Charlie Benante was blown away by Hetfield's performance: "I always thought of James as an exceptional guitar player and I always felt that when James played guitar it was as if he was expressing his emotions through the notes, as much as he was through his vocals. To me, I wish James played more leads, because to me his leads are incredibly emotional and different, and I can totally tell that it's him." Benante also had an opinion on Hetfield's newfound vocal harmony: "James wasn't originally what you'd classify as a rock singer, but as time went on people just adapted to that being his style and he became a singer."

Hetfield's views on faith and medicine were the subject of "The God That Failed"—more specifically, his thoughts on the ineffectiveness of faith.

The reception from critics combined surprise at the change in direction with satisfaction. It was by far the best Metallica had ever sounded on a record—which was a testament to Rock and his vision for the band. It became the benchmark for how metal albums should sound.

While other bands could imitate *Metallica's* sound, they couldn't mirror the songwriting of Hetfield and Ulrich, and Metallica stayed several steps ahead of the pack. With an album so approachable, they captured a significant chunk of mainstream listenership—previously reserved for the Bon Jovis, U2s and REMs of the world.

Metallica ploughed ahead into the *Billboard* charts like the juggernaut in the "Enter Sandman" video. For four consecutive weeks, the album sat at Number 1, proudly surveying its newly conquered kingdom—unheard of for a supposed extreme metal act.

The mainstream music press loved it—mainly because it was something they could relate to but also because they could comfortably discuss it with their readership. *Rolling Stone* said: "Several songs seemed destined to become hard rock classics. They've successfully bridged the gap between commercial metal and the much harder thrash of Slayer, Anthrax and Megadeth." The UK's *Q* magazine was equally praising: "[It] transformed them from cult metal heroes into global superstars . . . bringing a little refinement to their undoubted power." Pretty much everyone in print—from metal to men's lifestyle—recognized *Metallica* for what it was: a landmark in modern music. No band of this kind came close to replicating its impact.

With a monstrous album on their hands, Metallica were under pressure to deliver the goods on tour. Just as they had with ...*And Justice for All,* they hit the road before the album's release date. The Wherever I May Roam Tour exemplified their tireless touring habits. Kicking off in Petaluma, California, at the little known Phoenix Theater on July 1, the tour and its successor (Nowhere Else to Roam) kept the band on the road for the better part of three years—one of the most intense tour schedules in rock history.

The band took their enormous stage show to Europe. They played a show on Ulrich's childhood doorstep at the Gentofte Stadium in Denmark. Metallica returned to the Monsters of Rock festival in England, where the band dominated a bill that included Mötley Crüe, AC/DC and Queensrÿche.

One significant show took place at an airfield in Moscow, where Pantera were also on the bill. Pantera had been in the studio and didn't realize the significance that "The Black Album" would have for them. "It was us, The Black Crowes, Metallica and AC/DC," Brown recalled. "All I can remember is a sea of people, you couldn't count how many, and they all had flags of different countries. I remember that all James had for a backstage changing room was a tent!

"Anyway, when we got back we were laying down drum tracks for *Vulgar Display Of Power,* and then 'Enter Sandman' dropped," Brown continued. "Then we heard the rest of the record, and we said, 'Okay, we are going to make a heavier record every fuckin' time we go out.' That was the only way we felt we could top ourselves. Metallica gave us a spot to do that in, because they were all over the fuckin' radio with this thing, and they could have easily been shot dead because of it."

With radio going mad for their album, Metallica played a series of killer shows in the US that incorporated their famous "snake-pit" setup. Guests of the band and lucky fans got to view the gig from a sunken pit almost in the stage area.

Bob Nalbandian was there for one of the five nights the band played at the LA Forum. He recalled, "I was there with the guys from Armored Saint and I was sitting in the low section, and with the in-the-round setup James was sometimes fifty feet away." Nalbandian explained, "I remember the lights came on the audience, and I was sitting with my buddies when James looked right at me and shouted, 'Get off your ass!' and started laughing."

After the show, Nalbandian headed backstage. He said, "A guy taps me on the shoulder and it was James who looked at me and said, 'When I tell you to get off your ass, I mean get off your ass!' I was amazed he recognized me and James said, 'Sure, I knew it was you,' and we started talking about the old days."

October 12 saw the band return to Oakland for the Day on the Green concert, with support from Faith No More and Queensrÿche. It was a triumphant homecoming, with a frenzy similar to that memorable show in 1985. Eric Braverman was there and said, "That was one of the most kickass shows in the history of metal right there."

Chris Akin, one of the hosts of the *Classic Metal Show*—an excellent metal radio show with bases in Cleveland and Chicago—was also there. "It was awesome, any time you fence off the infield and turn it into a giant mosh pit—there's nothing wrong with that!" Akin recalled, referring to the Oakland Coliseum's baseball field.

Considering that people couldn't get enough of Metallica's new music, the remainder of 1991 and 1992 was taken up with huge touring commitments. Notable events along the way included an appearance at Wembley Stadium for the Freddie Mercury Tribute Concert on April 20 (the band had previously covered Queen's "Stone Cold Crazy") and the release of "Nothing Else Matters" as a single in May. Metallica toured with mega-selling Guns N' Roses, who were riding high on their double album, *Use Your Illusion I* and *II*.

Guns N' Roses and Metallica were the biggest heavy bands on the planet, so putting them on the same bill was a massive commercial draw. The band's paths had already crossed, at least on a social level. Both were hanging out in LA finishing albums, which led to all manner of drunken antics. Although Guns N' Roses often drew negative headlines for their debauched behavior, according to Ulrich, the Metallica guys were every bit as bad.

The shows did not go as planned. The sheer scale of operations—and the reality of being part of what was an increasingly "corporate" setup—apparently caused significant issues within the G N'R camp.

When James walked into an exploding pyrotechnic during a show at Montreal's Olympic Stadium on August 8, Metallica had a bigger issue on their hands. James's predicament could have been a lot worse, but as it was, he suffered serious burns to his left hand and arm. The show stopped while James was given medical treatment, and the confused crowd waited for the performance of Guns N' Roses. Singer Axl Rose then announced that he had throat problems and couldn't perform. That enraged the already frustrated crowd.

Thousands of dollars of damage later, the Olympic Stadium was cleared, after what could only be described as a riot. As he had in 1986, John Marshall stepped into Hetfield's rhythm guitar role for the shows that began on August 25—two weeks after the incident. To mark the significance of that near miss, Hetfield added a tattoo to his burned left arm that depicted flames, cards and the words "Carpe Diem Baby."

When the tour reached Seattle's Kingdome on October 6, 1992, the two biggest bands in rock parted company, seemingly on good terms, despite what had happened in Montreal. Metallica rolled into Europe, during which time two videos were released: *A Year and a Half in the Life of Metallica*, parts one and two. Essentially documenting the making of *Metallica*, these tapes had a significantly higher production standard than *Cliff 'Em All*. They featured footage from the early part of the Wherever I May Roam Tour, which officially ended in December 1992.

A show in Europe toward the end of the tour led to an interesting meeting between Megadeth's David Ellefson and Hetfield. "They were on 'The Black Album' tour and we were touring *Countdown to Extinction*. We ended up somewhere in Eastern Europe, maybe Budapest, and I hung out with James after the show." Ellefson explains, "I grew up hunting and with guns, and that subject was our common ground that we chatted about. James told me about hunting wild boar, and while the obvious thing would be to talk about music, I always find common ground on a more human level."

One would think that Mustaine's Megadeth in company with Metallica would have been an incendiary combination. According to Ellefson, however, controversial matters didn't come up: "There was that connection, but I never wanted to go there, knowing it could have been a touchy subject. And also, it was not my issue to ever talk about, so I avoided it."

1993 began much like 1992 ended, with more exhaustive touring, in North America and then Australia and the Far East. Afterward the band played some European gigs.

The tour emitted its final death rattle in July 1993. Given the amount of time the band had been on the road, one might expect Hetfield to have disappeared for months. On the contrary, he and Ulrich spent the next two months assembling a live package documenting the gargantuan trek that they had just finished. Metallica was relentless.

Entitled *Live Shit: Binge and Purge*, this souvenir/collector's edition included both audio and video footage of three shows from various points in the tour. The audio was recorded in Mexico City in 1993, while the concert footage was filmed in San Diego in 1991 and Seattle in 1989. The package was released in November 1993 and, despite being expensive, sold well. Hetfield spoke up about its hefty price tag: "If we put these things out separately over the years it would cost the same amount of money."

Regardless of the content—which included booklets, backstage passes, etc.—the price tag of more than $80 for the most basic version was quite steep. But it satisfied fans' need for new material, given how long it had been since *Metallica* had been released. The band hit the road again for a quick spin around North America on a jaunt called The Shit Hits the Sheds: Binging and Purging Across the USA. After this outing, Metallica retreated to the studio for an extended period of time.

After the unbelievable success of *Metallica* and the huge tours that supported it, the band took stock of where they stood in an industry that was always changing. The grunge movement had swept across the US and elsewhere, causing untold damage to some subgenres of heavy metal. Although by then the worst of that impact was over and Nirvana's Kurt Cobain, the movement's most identifiable figure, was dead, the damage inflicted on the rock world was telling. The onset of grunge meant that many thrash bands were driven underground or had to radically alter their sound to find an audience. The backlash against grunge in the mid-1990s meant that something new had to replace it, as well as fill the gaping holes in the metal industry resulting from its success.

That job fell to Pantera. Brown explained, "Metallica had gone and made the big rock record, and you had grunge and all that, so there was this big fuckin' empty space there. We just happened to be the guys with the songs and the perseverance to be the band to fill the gap with that grassroots fuckin' sound."

Brown was right on the money. While Metallica mixed in different and more commercial circles during much of the 1990s, Pantera kept gritty, thrash-orientated metal fires burning bright.

CHAPTER 11
CRUISE CONTROL

If Metallica had never released another record after "The Black Album," their legacy would be no worse off. Many fans would have been happy to call it quits after ...*And Justice for All.* For some critics and fans, the band that Metallica became—and the individuals the band members became after 1991—cannot be compared to the lean, hungry outfit that emerged from the metal underground in the 1980s.

Trips across America by U-Haul truck were replaced by blasts around the country by private jet. It would be difficult to suggest that privilege and availability of resources didn't have an effect on people. As much as anyone so successful may try to retain a semblance of normalcy, the scale of the beast makes that almost impossible on a day-to-day basis.

Before assessing where James Hetfield was in the mid-1990s, we need to acknowledge where he came from and the tough nature of his ascent. In the early days, Hetfield's musical evolution seemed to thrive in the face of adversity. He seemed to be driven by a desire to escape the bland normality of Downey. His upbringing and family situation encouraged him to better himself. It was only once the blur of the successful years had passed that he had time to focus on himself—though those days had not yet arrived. These were the days when the hard work was done.

On a personal level, it must have been hard to detach himself from the stage persona he was projecting and merely be himself. Considering his stage presence was fueled heavily by alcohol, he had a rather complex state of mind.

"When you've got fifteen thousand people yelling at you every night," opined Eric Braverman, "and all the weird stuff that goes with being in one of these bands, you are not a regular person. It's almost impossible to get a real insight into the kind of life James Hetfield has because almost all the perspectives are totally skewed, and therefore not readily relatable to normal people."

That may be stretching things a little, but life in a mega-selling rock band is not straightforward. Being in a secure financial position at a relatively young age would inevitably alter one's perspective.

On a personal level, the barriers that James put up as a young musician had not come down. If anything, the intrusion of the media and fans may have added to his distrust of people. Similarly, his desire to control everything around him—a habit linked to a defensive façade—was stronger than ever. This is part of what makes James Hetfield a genius.

"Most of the time, people who are in this rock 'n' roll business almost feel like they have to put on a show even when they are offstage," said Anthrax's Charlie Benante. "And that becomes increasingly hard to do, because at least when you are onstage you have a guitar or whatever in front of you, and you can easily portray that image up there. But once you are offstage and people continue to believe that you are that person, I think that's when life becomes a challenge."

If life was a challenge for James Hetfield, it didn't always seem that way. In February 1995, Hetfield, Ulrich and Hammett appeared on the KNAC metal radio station in Los Angeles. The station was closing down, and the guest DJ slot on February 15 was the last show. Rather fittingly, the last song played on the station was Metallica's "Fade to Black," which Hetfield introduced.

Later that month, Metallica, Bob Rock and Randy Staub went to Plant Studios in Sausalito, California, to begin work on Metallica's sixth studio album, *Load*.

In the spring of 1995, the band were in a rich vein of creativity and there was significantly more material than would be used for one album. That might have been because the studio location allowed more family access or because long periods on the road had provided new inspiration. Either way, everything was going well on the surface. With the seemingly settled production team of Hetfield, Ulrich and Rock able to do no wrong, the future for Metallica looked bright.

The band escaped for some live shows, called the Escape from the Studio Tour, which kicked off on August 23 at the now demolished London Astoria. Compared to some places the band had played during the previous three years, it was like seeing Metallica in your living room. Tickets were only available to fan club members. Metallica ripped through a feral set that ranked as high as any in their live history. Even Hetfield—who was sporting a new mullet haircut—acknowledged the amazing atmosphere in that sweaty hall. Two new songs, "2 x 4" and "Devil's Dance," were swallowed up in a frenzy of band-love that night.

The band disappeared into the studio again. They only emerged with any great intent on December 14, when they honored Motörhead's Lemmy by playing at his 50th birthday celebrations at the Whisky in Los Angeles.

The early part of 1996 was quiet on the Metallica front. For James Hetfield, it was a difficult time. His father, Virgil, whom he had gradually seen more of, had been suffering from cancer and passed away early that year. In a moving interview with *So What,* Hetfield spoke highly of his father. He said that it was only in later years that he realized the large part his dad had played in his life and how much influence he had had on him. When they became closer later in life, Hetfield realized they had similar interests. When Virgil became ill, James admired his strength. While admitting to "battling" the ideology of Christian Science as a teenager and in his twenties, Hetfield realized how "magical and powerful" the faith was in his father's mind during his fight against cancer.

Given Hetfield's admission, it seems that he had not slammed the door in the face of religion completely after his mother's death. While he did not actively embrace its doctrines, he didn't entirely dismiss Christian Science and its concepts and principles stayed with him. Considering what James was doing in his 20s, it's astounding to see that he likely still gave more than the occasional thought to religion. If only speculation, this information is fascinating considering Hetfield's distinctly rebellious attitude and his use of the word "battled," which suggests that religion was much closer to the surface than suspected.

Meanwhile, Ulrich announced that the album was progressing and that some of the lyrical content might surprise listeners. Hetfield's open discussion with *So What* about his father's passing should have given some clue as to his deep introspection.

One could speculate that Hetfield was considerably more receptive to feelings of regret and nostalgia regarding his childhood and early adult life. It would remain to be seen whether this emotional state would manifest itself in his lyrics and songwriting or whether *Load* was capable of replicating the commercial success of "The Black Album." Metallica announced that their sixth studio album would be released on June 3, 1996.

Before appraising Hetfield and Metallica's musical legacy of the 1995-1997 era, it's important to make one fact clear. Despite any claims to the contrary and regardless of how Hetfield felt emotionally, the influences that drove *Load* and its successor, *Reload*, were all his.

Yes, the band had a little input—mostly on a lyrical level—but the genres of music that spawned the thirty or so tracks that appeared over the next two years had more to do with Hetfield and less to do with Ulrich, Newsted and Hammett. Hetfield had always been a country music fan and an admirer of its accompanying lifestyle. You only need to look at his hobbies—hunting, motorbikes and drag racing—to know he was much more in sync with that lifestyle than with Ulrich's more cultured European mindset. The material that the band came up with had his ethos branded all over it.

What the press did not expect during the *Load* promo tour was the band's bizarre new look. Fashion per se had never been high on the agenda for Metallica, Hetfield previously seemed to revel in his unkempt and hirsute appearance, reminiscent of a young Ted Nugent, but for this album he had short black hair and wore pinstripe suit trousers in the press shots. The rest of the band were much the same as we'd come to know them, sporting various attire complete with some makeup and, in Hammett's case, a lip ring.

The press and fans had no idea what to make of Hetfield's new image, and it seemed astounding that the band behind "Damage, Inc." and "Battery" could ever be dressed up like this. The band members themselves seemed unconcerned as to what anyone thought. The press shots in question were taken by revered Dutch photographer Anton Corbijn of U2 and Depeche Mode photographic fame.

The fact that Corbijn was a fashion photographer said a lot about where Metallica thought they stood in the world. Their egos were massaged thoroughly by all the adulation their fame had brought them. This would all be okay, of course, if the music still stood up to scrutiny.

Before a note of *Load* was heard, Hetfield was conspicuously quick to defend the new look, as he told the Metallica website www.metallicworld.co.uk: "People freak out about things that are different. Five years [since the release of *Metallica*] is a long time. Nirvana came and went. A lot of things happened in that five years."

What was also surfacing was an apparent shift towards bad temper by Hetfield, as Ulrich told *Rolling Stone*: "The other day, we were talking about some song title, and there was something that didn't make sense. We were standing in the kitchen at the studio. I'm going, 'What does this mean?' And he goes, 'Fuck all this. I don't know what the fuck this all means. Jesus Christ!' Bark, bark, bark! Then he storms out of the room and leaves the studio. I'm just standing there laughing."

The release of the unusual first single "Until It Sleeps" on May 20 did nothing to allay the fears of the band's hardcore following. Reputedly a song about James's father's battle with cancer, it sent alarm bells ringing with its overtly commercial feel.

A listening party was held at the Dynamo Festival in Holland on May 28. The entire album was aired through the public address system and received mixed responses.

A week later, *Load* made its worldwide appearance on record store shelves. It featured a controversial cover image entitled "Blood and Semen" by photographer Andres Serrano, whose work often used body fluids as a medium.

*Load*s cover featured a new, softer Metallica logo. While Serrano's garish artwork and Corbijn's liner photos of the band in makeup were not for the squeamish, perhaps the fourteen songs that made up the seventy-nine minutes of *Load* were.

The most controversial track on *Load* was the country ballad "Mama Said." For some fans, the song signaled an abrupt end to their relationship with Metallica. For others, it was a poignant ode to Hetfield's mother and should have been taken precisely for what it was. Vocally, it is a strong and convincing performance, and while the thought of Hetfield delivering such a delicate message is initially jarring, it works very well. For radio audiences it was another acceptable Metallica incarnation.

Hetfield explained how the song evolved on www.metallicaworld. co.uk, saying it was written on an electric guitar and was not intended for anyone else to hear. He pointed out the country tinges and admitted that he was heavily into that style of music. "I guess people were taken by the openness of it," he suggested.

Renowned author and journalist Malcolm Dome defended Hetfield's position: "I think he took on the mantle that Cliff had, which is the person who wasn't just the metal-head, but was prepared to listen to country, Southern rock—lots of different kinds of music. And I think he's had that input in some of the band's better years."

Other highlights include the lengthy closer "The Outlaw Torn": a sprawling epic not unlike "Bleeding Me." Amusingly, Ulrich suggested that this was the greatest heavy metal song ever written.

Despite *Load* being the least invigorating collection of songs that Metallica had ever assembled, the music press hailed it as a success. Like its superior predecessor, *Load* spent four weeks at number one on the *Billboard* chart. *Entertainment Weekly* said, "[The album] captures the band's earnest pursuit of its Sisyphean mission: to create hard rock that reaches grownups and basement-dwelling teens." *The New York Times* saw it as a success: "On *Load*, Metallica has altered its music, learning new skills. Hetfield has committed himself to melodies, carrying tunes where he used to bark, and he no longer sounds sheepish when he sings quietly." *Melody Maker* perhaps captured the feeling best: "A Metallica album is traditionally an exhausting event. It should rock you to exhaustion, leave you brutalized and drained. This one is no exception. It is, however, the first Metallica album to make me wonder at any point, 'What the fuck was that?' It's as if the jackboot grinding the human face were to take occasional breaks for a pedicure."

Although *Load* was well received, it did not sound like a "proper" Metallica album. The band were well aware of this, and Hetfield defended the album in an interview in Australia: "I really hope that they [the fans] can understand what we are up to. I hope that they can follow through with us." Hetfield realized that both the band's image and their new direction would divide the fans. His comments even hinted that Hetfield felt that *Load*'s loose style might have taken things too far.

On a stylistic level, *Load* was a response to some of the more rigid arrangements that they'd been bound by previously, particularly on *...And Justice for All*. If they'd made this super-loose, biker rock album immediately after *...And Justice for All*, it might have been career-threatening. Because of the enormous commercial success of *Metallica*, the band could go wherever they wanted musically, and this detour was the result. They had bought their freedom, and they made full use of that luxury.

Author Joel McIver—while not a huge fan of the album's music—understood what the band were attempting: "I think they tried a few different directions with the honest intention of exploring new territory, but those ideas simply didn't work."

Testament's Chuck Billy was far from convinced by *Load*. He explained, "The whole band got to contribute on the *Load* record, and at that point I decided that James had to sing his own lyrics [for the best results]. When you sing your own lyrics, you sing them with more conviction and belief. When I heard that record it sounded to me like it wasn't him . . . and it wasn't the James that I knew. There was none of the clever lyrics and clever parts and it changed how I felt about their music."

Pantera's Rex Brown benefited from Metallica's deviation, and he didn't give *Load* a second thought. He said, "All that makeup and shit? I really didn't know what to think. I didn't even care because by that time we were headlining arenas. It wasn't the brand of shit we were doing, and we kind of took over that spot where they left off."

As far as seeing James and the band around, Brown was bemused about the circles Metallica were running in: "We only saw them spasmodically, but when we did, Lars would come in with fuckin' John McEnroe! You know, it was crazy. I don't think James was hanging out with all these artsy fuckin' dudes, though. He's not that kind of guy."

To date *Load* has sold in excess of five million copies in the US alone. Despite resistance from a few camps, by anyone else's standards, *Load's* sales figures represent colossal success. For Metallica it was a sideways step—hardly a surprise given the untouchable precedent "The Black Album" had set. A bigger concern was the musical conundrum posed by *Load* and how it could be followed. Was thrash gone forever? Was this new look here to stay?

Only time would tell, but in the meantime, the band went out on tour. Two fan club shows got the ball rolling on June 23 and 24, followed by a spot on the summer Lollapalooza tour, which featured Soundgarden, Rancid and the Ramones, among others.

With one grunge act and two punk outfits in the upper echelons of the lineup, some questioned Metallica's role in such a non-metal bill. Some added that fact to *Load's* non-metal pretenses and concluded that Metallica had deserted their metal roots. Hetfield jumped to his band's defense when quizzed on their exact motives: "We did Lollapalooza because we wanted to and it was cool. It was as simple as that. We got to see a few great bands and make some new friends. We played in front of some people who came to see us and some people who wouldn't normally listen to us."

Although Lollapalooza was a success, it was more significant in that Newsted traveled separately from his bandmates. This was indicative of some festering differences of opinion between Hetfield and Newsted. Although *Load* had been more of a band effort in some ways, Newsted had no writing credits on it, which raised a few eyebrows given his ten-year tenure in the band. This issue of freedom to create might not have amounted to much in 1996, but as time went on it became a bigger problem, as Hetfield increasingly tightened his grip on the band's extracurricular activities.

The Poor Touring Me European cycle through familiar cities and the release of the poppy "Hero of the Day" as a single took up late September. This new, radio-friendly Metallica sound was lapped up by mainstream audiences. More autumn dates in the UK and Europe brought the band back to London to appear on the *Later with Jools Holland* show, where Hetfield performed a rather nervous version of "Mama Said," while his bandmates joined him for "Wasting My Hate" and "King Nothing."

A video featuring Hetfield wearing a cowboy hat—while sitting in the back of a taxi strumming a guitar—accompanied the release of "Mama Said" as a single on November 18. Although it was a new look, it was one that he carried rather well—certainly more so than the awkward, dapper image that heralded the album release.

A mainstream audience identified with a mellower Metallica sound, and the single did well on the charts. Touring continued into the first half of 1997, with a brief interruption for Ulrich's marriage to Skylar Satinstein. Hetfield performed best man duties, although the event was only acknowledged the following night at the American Music Awards, where the band received an award for Best Metal/Hard Rock Album.

Hetfield was in a steady relationship with Francesca Tomasi—a former member of the band's behind-the-scenes team. After the tour finished in May, the band had a couple of spare months, and Hetfield tied the knot with Francesca on August 17.

The *Load* sessions were a very productive time in the studio—with more tracks recorded than could fit on one studio album. After Hetfield's wedding and some festival dates in Europe, it was announced that a follow-up to *Load* would be released in November, consisting of more songs from the same recording sessions.

"We wrote 27 songs for *Load* and were developing it as a double album," Lars explained to *Billboard* magazine. "We then got the offer [in January 1996] to play Lollapalooza [that summer] and [decided] we [would] put one record out now with most of the songs that are done and then we [would] come back after a year and finish the rest of them. As far as I'm concerned, you can take any of these songs and interchange them on the two albums. . . . We didn't want to leave it lying around for three years and worry about what it would sound like when we came back to it."

Prior to the new album's release, Metallica performed two acoustic sets at an event organized by Neil Young to raise funds for the Bridge School for disabled children in San Francisco. It was appropriate that Young was the organizer, as he had some similarities with Hetfield. "Mama Said" wasn't far off from the style Young specialized in. The same applied to "Low Man's Lyric," a new track the band released, which had almost a bluegrass feel to it. Jerry Cantrell of Alice in Chains joined the band onstage as they covered Lynyrd Skynyrd's anthemic "Tuesday's Gone."

Cantrell always had a strong affinity with Hetfield, as he explained: "James is top of the heap to me. He always has been. I admire the way that he chooses to live and his fingerprint is absolutely all over the band and its music." It was an evening full of energetic performances, including from Lou Reed, the Smashing Pumpkins and Alanis Morissette. The event became an annual fixture.

Many fans' excitement was tempered by the release of *Reload*'s first single, "The Memory Remains." Anyone who hoped *Load* had been but a mid-career wobble and that the band would get back on track was disappointed. Some considered this new track to be worse than most of the songs on *Load*, and the weird collaboration with singer Marianne Faithful highlighted the song's lack of imagination. Two free shows, one at a parking lot in Philadelphia and another at a London dance venue called Ministry of Sound, ushered in the release of *Reload*.

"It's the second half of *Load*," Ulrich told *Metal Edge* magazine. "Only it's coming out a year and a half later."

Reload was nothing more than *Load*'s poor relation, and no amount of advertising, gimmickry or defense from the band could change that. Given how unsatisfactory *Load* was deemed on some fronts, the suggestion that its successor was worse was really saying something.

Hetfield's response was understandably defensive: "We liked the songs, and we wanted to get back into the studio after less of a tour. A lot of them needed a little work . . . and I think at the end of the day, it's us pleasing ourselves. We're selfish bastards, and have been since day one, and that's how we've stayed pure and how we've kind of lasted all this time."

Reload hit stores on November 17, 1997. The cover continued *Load*s fascination with body fluids. It featured another abstract Serrano image, this time substituting urine for semen.

On balance, *Reload* was very similar to *Load*. *Reload* did have a couple of decent moments. One has to question the rationale behind releasing both instead of one album containing the "best" of the two. Reviews by mainstream magazines were extremely positive. *Rolling Stone* called it as they saw it, although their assessment that the music was "strongly rooted in the group's apocalyptic metal sound" was strange. *Musician* was even more dramatic when it said "greasy, driving, full of fat grooves, lyric and rhythmic hooks, and sonic curveballs . . . [it] captures one of rock's greatest bands at its peak."

Both magazines overstated matters, but those reviews showed that Metallica's audience had become considerably more mainstream since 1991. The fact that a relatively conservative music press was praising the material suggested that a huge shift had taken place. *Load* and *Reload* were as good—or as bad—as each other, depending on where you stand. *Reload* sold almost five million copies in the US and occupied the Number 1 spot on the *Billboard* chart.

Brian Slagel—a long-term ally of the band—appreciated the *Load* and *Reload* era: "The band was listening to a lot of 1970s metal at the time, so the albums were influenced by that stuff and not the NWOBHM stuff they had been influenced [by] before. I really like *Load* a lot and think there are some great songs on it. Also, Bob Rock had more influence on them, as he was more into the rock 'n' roll stuff."

Jason Newsted said in one article that he was uncomfortable with the photographs and artwork—although he qualified that by saying he later grew to like the cover art as a "positive" sentiment using the two life forces of blood and semen.

"The band was totally out of touch with their fans" was Braverman's less encouraging opinion. That posed an interesting question: Who *were* Metallica's fans in 1997?

Their fan base was in transition—something that had been happening since "The Black Album" catapulted the band into the living rooms of the world. While some die-hard thrash fans from the early days hung on and hoped for a return to the heavy stuff, others deserted the band for harder alternatives. While that erosion took place, a new demographic of Metallica fans climbed on board. The sound of *Load* and *Reload* was arguably perfect for their tastes—contrary to the suggestion that the band was detached from their fan base.

While the two albums were a sonic departure, they reflected where the band were at and attracted the appropriate listenership. Both albums sold a ton of units, which says a lot about the band's cross-spectrum appeal during the late 1990s.

CHAPTER 12
BACK TO THE GARAGE

While the *Load* and *Reload* saga represented transition for Metallica and their millions of fans, the period was a pivotal time in James Hetfield's life. His father's death, followed by his marriage must have put him in a new emotional place, which was reflected in his creative output.

While these two records were far from Metallica's best, they offered some clear views into Hetfield's soul. They allowed him to play the kind of music that he *personally* enjoyed—with no need to fear the consequences.

Country, blues and Southern rock have always been key components in Hetfield's musical makeup. At some point in a long career, those influences were going to come out. So it might as well have been when a negative response would be the least damaging. Considering Hetfield had attracted a new type of fan, you could mark the era a success—unless, of course, you are a fan of pure thrash metal.

1998 began with another Metallica wedding, as Kirk Hammett tied the knot in Hawaii with Lani Grutadauro. The release of the popular "Unforgiven II" on March 3 heralded the beginning of another intense tour, with the Poor Touring Me Tour reaching Australia in April. James Hetfield had other developments going on in his life, too, with the birth of his first daughter, Cali Tee Hetfield, on June 11, 1998. Hetfield flew back to California and was present for her birth.

After two weeks at home, James was back on the tour, which swung through the East Coast en route to Texas. With sold-out shows and enthusiastic responses to the new songs, Metallica still commanded huge box-office success. "Fuel" was released as a single on July 4 before the tour came to a pause in San Diego in the middle of September.

The band went into the studio to record cover songs for an album called *Garage Inc.* The release was promoted with a series of small club shows, with a Metallica tribute band named Battery. The double-album's first disc features the newly recorded covers and the second showcases much of what had surfaced on *Garage Days Re-Revisited*, plus some B-sides.

Of the new material, versions of tracks by Diamond Head ("It's Electric"), Black Sabbath ("Sabbra Cadabra") and Mercyful Fate (a medley including "Satan's Fall," "Curse of the Pharaohs," "Corpse Without a Soul," "Into the Coven" and "Evil") were logical choices to rework. Less obvious were Nick Cave's "Loverman," Bob Seger's "Turn the Page" and Thin Lizzy's "Whisky in the Jar," although the latter fit in with Hetfield's high regard for Phil Lynott's poetic lyrical abilities. Released on November 23, *Garage Inc.* has a cover image featuring the band members looking like grease-monkeys at an auto shop.

Lars Ulrich was keen to point out how much more relaxed the process of making the album had been. "It's definitely easier to work with other people's material," he said in an article called "Garage Days" on www.metallicaworld.co.uk: "We like to turn them into something very Metallica, different than how the original artist did it. You don't get so fucking anal about it, and you can bang these covers out in like five minutes."

The critical response to what was essentially an intriguing space-filler was very positive, with most recognizing that the band wanted to identify their broad range of influences. *Garage Inc.* sold in excess of five million copies—hardly poor numbers for a covers collection.

Rolling Stone said, "Gloriously hard as the album is, you can't miss Metallica's good-natured side coming through." *Entertainment Weekly* felt similarly, saying, "We'll have to wait until Metallica's next 'proper' album to find out if this trip to the garage recharges their batteries. Still, all things considered, *Garage Inc.* is an intermittently exhilarating joyride."

The band put out a live DVD package on the same day called *Cunning Stunts*. Featuring an unusually dull live performance of the band from the *Load* tour and a broad spread of material from across the years, this DVD fell flat in the eyes of many fans.

The awards kept coming in early 1999, with the band bagging another Grammy in the category of Best Metal Performance for one of *Reload*s brighter moments, "Better Than You." Metallica's cover of Thin Lizzy's timeless "Whiskey in the Jar" was released as a single.

Shortly afterward the band was honored at the Recording Industry Association of America show, with a much coveted Diamond Award in recognition of 10 million sales of *Metallica*. April 7, 1999, was officially declared "Metallica Day" in San Francisco—an amazing coup for any act, especially a heavy metal group.

April 1999 saw a new direction for the band, one whose roots lay in an orchestral score of "Nothing Else Matters" by composer Michael Kamen. While the band resisted putting in too much of Kamen's orchestral arrangement back in 1991, there was another version nicknamed "The Elevator Version"—featuring far more of Kamen's lavish orchestration. At the time, Kamen had made a throwaway remark to Hetfield about arranging and composing a full concert combining Metallica with a full-blown orchestra. While the response was positive and the band liked what Kamen had done with the alternate version of "Nothing Else Matters," considerable time passed before Kamen finally received a phone call from Q Prime's Peter Mensch saying words to the effect, "Metallica will do that concert you talked about." Kamen was seemingly astounded that the idea was still under consideration, but he was enthused.

This wasn't a new concept for Kamen, as he'd already had orchestral dalliances with giants of popular music like Deep Purple and Eric Clapton. In terms of sheer ambition, a venture of this kind with Metallica would eclipse all of that.

The plan was to marry Metallica with the San Francisco Symphony Orchestra and release a double live album and accompanying DVD entitled *S&M*. Hetfield told *Rolling Stone* how the project came about: "Maestro Kamen came to us with the idea almost two years ago. He had done projects with other rock people, like David Bowie, Eric Clapton and Pink Floyd. He wanted to get a little more extreme, so he chose us.

I'm sure there's something more extreme—he could have picked, like, Graveworm—but I think we were a pretty good choice. We said, 'Hell, yeah.' You don't pass these things up. It took two years to pull together—from the initial idea to deciding which orchestra to picking the songs."

The band were still involved with the Poor Re-Touring Me jaunt, with support from Monster Magnet, but April 21 and 22 were set aside to record with the orchestra at the Berkeley Community Theater. The two shows were recorded before the band took off for Mexico and South America, prior to swinging back through Europe with added backup from Mercyful Fate and Apocalyptica. The Finnish group Apocalyptica consisted of classically trained cellists with their own unique take on Metallica songs.

European commitments wore on until July, when the band returned to New York to perform at Woodstock. Metallica's set was marred by considerable violence—a regrettable feature of the event as a whole. Instead of being a celebration of a famous musical gathering, Woodstock 1999 was a bad-tempered riot.

November 23, 1999, saw the release of *S&M* and the rock world held its breath, given that this was such an ambitious move. The band promoted the album release by doing similar shows accompanied by orchestras in Berlin and New York City.

The primary concern was that an orchestra was involved; this was acceptable as far as most metal fans were concerned. It was more of an issue whether the orchestral arrangements would complement Metallica's diverse set.

What is different about *S&M* is that on a production level, the record was made very rapidly—by Metallica's standards at least. While

Bob Rock was still behind the controls, his input was less than it would have been on studio records, and Kamen's arrangements dictated matters significantly. Both are credited on the sleeve notes.

S&M begins with Metallica's familiar intro, Ennio Morricone's "Ecstasy of Gold," and immediately the benefits of a large orchestra are clear. Whereas the traditional prerecorded intro sounded tinny and almost clichéd, this new incarnation sounds majestic and is the perfect precursor to such a dramatic amalgam of worlds. "The Call of Ktulu," with Hetfield's mesmerizing, clean intro, benefited similarly.

Kamen managed to get the two components—Metallica and the orchestra—to complement each other. Sadly, things go a little wrong on "Master of Puppets." Maybe it came too early in the set, or possibly the track was too complex. The band and the orchestra did little more than battle each other throughout, rendering this live version inferior to its studio original. "Of Wolf and Man" from "The Black Album" follows, and while it isn't an obvious selection, it works out well.

Perhaps *S&M*'s best moment is the first of two new tracks written specifically for the album, "No Leaf Clover." While closely linked in style to much of the *Load* and *Reload* material, it benefits from the monstrous assistance this type of presentation offers. It features a curiously mainstream Hetfield vocal style, one which other band members—particularly Newsted—had doubts about, according to the *S&M* documentary. "Hero of the Day," "Devil's Dance" and "Bleeding Me" come next and are adequate renditions of the originals, as the first half of the album draws to a close.

S&M closes with four integral parts of the band's back catalog. By and large they work well—largely because they are great songs that stand up anywhere. Of the four, "Sad But True" is the weakest, whereas "One," "Enter Sandman" and "Battery" sound very loyal to the originals.

The problem with *S&M* is consistency, which means that the band is always recovering from a weak moment or falling flat from a strong one. On some occasions, the band and orchestra do not sync. However, fans of the band were enthusiastic and Metallica enjoyed the experience. *S&M* is also notable because it is the last album that Newsted appears on.

As with most of Metallica's output, the response of the music press was supportive, with many recognizing the ambitious nature of the project and tailoring their reviews accordingly. *Rolling Stone* went over the top when they said the record "creates the most crowded, ceiling-rattling basement rec room in rock . . . [in its] sheer awesomeness . . . the performance succeeds . . . the monster numbers benefit from supersizing. The effect is . . . one of timelessness."

Britain's *Q* magazine was a little more cautious, suggesting, "another just about forgivable flirtation with Spinal Tap-esque lunacy . . . a fine hit-heavy live LP with bolted-on bombast from the S.F. Symphony . . . Michael Kamen's scores swoop and soar with impressive portent throughout."

In some ways, *S&M* restored fans' faith in the band after the confusion of *Load* and *Reload*. But not everyone was convinced. "*S&M* was a misguided thing," suggested Dome. "It was an interesting idea, but I don't really think that the band and the orchestra connected, apart from on the new songs. Otherwise, it was a band playing the songs the way they know how, with the orchestra having to fit in where they could."

Sales were good, and with the band on a high at the end of 1999, they powered towards the Millennium on the M2K Tour, accompanied by Kid Rock and Sevendust. The year culminated in Detroit with a show supported by Ted Nugent, which became known as the Whiplash Bash. Metallica were still at the top of the pile.

For Metallica, the year 2000 was nothing but problematic. Having survived the 1990s with their credibility intact, they were about to be put in a position that tested the loyalty of their huge fan base. Bizarrely, it wouldn't be the actual music that caused the problem but rather the way the music was used and distributed.

In early 2000, Metallica recorded the single "I Disappear," an average tune in truth, which was intended to appear on the soundtrack for the blockbuster movie *Mission: Impossible 2*. Bootleg versions of "I Disappear" were heard on various radio stations months before the actual soundtrack was due for release. The version that aired was not the one that was due to appear on the movie's accompanying album. The source of the material turned out to be the Internet, where songs in digital file form could be easily shared and distributed.

One of the main exponents of this file-sharing phenomenon was Napster, which allowed users to register and search for free music files online. The implications for the music industry were huge, because this bypassed the sales process and the music became freely available. Metallica saw this as too big a threat. In April 2000 the band took legal action against Napster and three collaborating American universities, with the main thrust of the action based on the infringement of the band's copyright.

What followed over the next few months was a gargantuan legal battle. Lars Ulrich championed the Metallica cause against Napster—and not the 300,000 users who'd been identified as having downloaded free Metallica songs.

Hetfield's role was very much backseat, although he was supportive of the action. He said, "We are going after Napster, the main
artery. We are not going after the individual fans." Clearly this was
an attempt to appease the hordes, but Hetfield made it clear that
Metallica would not tolerate such infringement of their rights.

Ulrich held off furious fans, who felt betrayed by their heroes for
not letting them download their music for free. What was lost on some
fans was that Ulrich was entitled to defend his and his band's creative
output, given that file-sharing was illegal. James was at home with his
family following the birth of his second child, Castor Virgil Hetfield.
He was probably happy to be out of the limelight, although Ulrich's
popularity as the band's spokesman was declining and that of Metallica
soon followed.

In June, the band took off on The Summer Sanitarium Tour. That
must have been a relief given the fan uproar. Kicking off on the East
Coast, the tour proved eventful and tragic, with the death of a fan who
fell from an upper balcony at a show in Baltimore, Maryland. Hetfield
was in the wars, too, injuring some discs in his back, which caused him
to miss three shows in early July. Help came from an amalgam of artists like Korn, System of a Down and Kid Rock, who performed some
Metallica songs.

The tour continued with Hetfield, but the Napster issue loomed
large. Early August marked the end of the tour, and Hetfield's public
business with the band for the year was largely done.

In a *Playboy* interview in 2001, Hetfield explained his feelings
about Lars taking charge of the war against Napster: "My wife and I
were giving birth to a second child. And family is *number one*. So Lars

had to run with the torch, and there were a few bad moves. You know, Lars can get really mouthy and be a snotty-nosed kid at times. I cringed at certain interviews: 'Oh dude, don't say that.'"

The year 2000 ended with the Napster issue unresolved. Metallica was also dealing with several other lawsuits, including one against a perfume company for calling one of their products Metallica. Why any company would call a product such a name is amusing, but Metallica were not amused. The year was over, and they had survived it—just about. While the Napster issue rumbled on, intra-band issues that had been bubbling under the surface for some time now began to pose more immediate problems.

CHAPTER 13

PLAYBOY

The New Year began dramatically for Metallica fans, with the shocking announcement in mid-January that Jason Newsted was quitting the band. The main reason Newsted gave was that he risked causing his body physical harm by continuing. That reason was plausible, particularly since Newsted had back problems—his energetic onstage style was physically demanding. However, many observers thought this was just one factor and speculated a breakdown in communication with James Hetfield may have also been a contributing factor.

When Newsted joined the band, his friend Eric Braverman questioned what would happen if and when he stood up to Hetfield. While there had been occasional rumblings of discontent, as well as the absence of many Newsted writing credits, it had never come to a head. The reason it did now likely had to do with Newsted's own decision to be more vocal, rather than any change in Hetfield.

While Newsted obviously wasn't thrilled with the Metallica environment, it came out later that much of his frustration hinged on Hetfield's intolerance of any projects outside Metallica. (Hetfield had done a few himself over the years—he appeared on some Corrosion of Conformity albums and a couple of other projects—but these were low-key affairs and he did not promote his involvement.) Newsted was part of a side-project called Echobrain—a pop-rock act that sounded nothing whatsoever like Metallica.

While Metallica had suggested that they would head into the studio "sometime soon," Newsted was not keen to sit around and do nothing. He threw himself into the Echobrain project without even considering that it would be an issue.

For Hetfield, it *was* an issue—so much so that he said that it was not acceptable for band members to do their own thing outside of Metallica. At the time of Newsted's departure, this information was slow to emerge. On the surface, it just looked as if the natural time for Newsted to move on had arrived. The official biography on the band's website stated, "No one reason can be fairly the cause, more several long-standing issues that silently grew beyond their initial molehills."

In an interview with Joel McIver soon after his departure, Newsted seemed happy with his decision, albeit a little unclear and evasive about some of the more personal issues involved. When asked if it was solely about looking after his body, Newsted threw in a few scraps that suggested there were other factors. "I wasn't confident I could be the '110%' dude performer that people know me as, and I needed to have that. And now that I've had a year to think about it, I think that . . .

James, where he was in his headspace, you know, at that time, with his personal life and different things."

Even from such a cryptic explanation, it was obvious Newsted still had great respect for Hetfield—and recognized his importance in holding Metallica together. It would be a while until the real story came out, and there was much speculation regarding Newsted's replacement.

Joey Vera was a name that came up as a possible replacement, just as it had fourteen years earlier. Newsted felt that whoever replaced him needed to be not just a seasoned player but also someone who could deal with the bigger Metallica issues. Vera certainly fit that bill, at least in Newsted's opinion, and the fact that he was well known to Hetfield and Ulrich made him one of the more obvious choices. Vera's career with Armored Saint—while moderately successful—could never be likened to the success of Metallica, so it was an opportunity that might have suited both parties in 2001. He wasn't the only choice, and over the next few months, several bass players' names were touted around.

The Napster issue was an ongoing ordeal for Ulrich and Metallica's battery of legal representation, but the band was winning the battle, given that a court had agreed with certain key aspects of the case. While Ulrich took the reins on this matter, Hetfield remained relatively low profile in the legal and press discussions.

A major interview appeared in the March 5 issue of *Playboy* magazine, where the band members—including Newsted—revealed some of the most insightful information the public had ever heard. It wasn't a conventional interview, as all four members were interviewed separately. The results were depressing and gave huge clues that relations had not been good in the band for some time.

While Ulrich's interview focused on Napster and wider band issues, the other three took things down a more personal route, with Hammett particularly effusive about some of the more unpleasant aspects of his upbringing. For Hetfield, the most revealing information was about his alcohol consumption. "I had to have a bottle of vodka just for fun. I'm surprised I'm still alive," Hetfield told Ron Tannebaum, who was conducting the interview.

Newsted had something to say about Hetfield's drinking habits, too. "James is the only one that ever drank so much that he couldn't show up for a rehearsal or for photos. He is the only one who actually poisoned himself," he said.

While Hetfield's drinking habits were well known, there was a sense that they had become a bigger issue. It wasn't that James was unaware. He had attempted to address the matter himself by briefly seeking therapy during the *Load* era. He explained, "I took more than a year off from drinking—and the skies didn't part. It was just life, but less fun. . . . The evil didn't come out. I wasn't laughing, wasn't having a good time. I realized drinking is a part of me. Now I know how far to go . . . I wouldn't say that I'm an alcoholic—but then, you know, alcoholics never say they're alcoholics."

When the subject turned to Newsted and intra-band tension, Hetfield's sense of humor quickly disappeared. He couldn't relate to why anyone would want to do anything outside of Metallica, and he felt that doing so would detract from what Metallica were all about. Newsted would have said that all he did was entertain himself creatively while his primary concern, Metallica, were on a break between albums. Newsted had apparently argued vehemently that Echobrain wouldn't compromise his involvement with Metallica. In *Playboy* he stated very clearly, "I would not leave Metallica for another band. If I ever happened to choose that path, I would do it to live my life, not depart to play in another band."

Hetfield did not see it that way. In the same interview, Hammett said, "James demands loyalty and unity, and I respect that . . ." Hammett added, "I think it's morally wrong to keep someone away from what keeps him happy."

Newsted had the most to say. He felt that Hetfield was being unfair by exerting such rigid control and that he had double standards. "James is on quite a few records: in the *South Park* movie, when Kenney goes to hell, James is singing, and he's on just about every Corrosion of Conformity album," Newsted complained. "I can't play my shit, but he can go play with other people."

But what of Hetfield's position? It's easy to criticize the man and suggest that his view of extracurricular activity was to blame. Without Hetfield's strength of character and strong sense of unity, would Metallica have been so monstrously successful?

Few would argue that in order to hold such an entity together, a strong person needs to be in charge and deal with the vast array of personal dynamics that arise from living and working in a massive rock band. There's a need for an able communicator and "face," and those were two roles that Hetfield and Ulrich, respectively, had gravitated towards.

While both current and former band members had plenty to say about Hetfield's hardline approach, it was vital to the survival of the band. His desire to influence every aspect of Metallica was never to the detriment of the band's progress and success.

The band tried to put a positive spin on events, as Hetfield commented at the ESPN Action Sports and Music Awards: "We're really enjoying each other's company and retouching on things we haven't connected on in a long time. It's a fun and healthy time for us."

It's unclear what those "things" were. Although Ulrich mentioned on the Metallica website that the band felt no particular pressure on a musical level, he made no mention of this period being a particularly harmonious one.

The Napster issue dominated Ulrich's thoughts, and the band lost many fans—rightly or wrongly. Few would question that Metallica's decision to sue Napster was the right approach—and that it nipped the concept of illegal file-sharing in the bud for the benefit of other acts. But for Metallica's critics, it was the *way* that they did it that grated.

Metallica entered their recording space in San Francisco with Bob Rock to record new material. The location of the studio was the Presidio—a former army barracks and a different environment from anywhere they had worked before. This was intentional, of course. It was a conscious effort to change from the comfortable studio environments of the past. It was hoped that the results would be similarly uncomfortable.

Eric Braverman was familiar with the venue. "It's the most expensive real estate in the world maybe," Braverman suggested. "They all have their own individual offices in there and shit."

Nothing was heard from the band until two months later, when it was announced that the war with Napster was essentially over and that a compromise was reached out of court. The press release said, "The settlement will enable the parties to work together to make Napster a positive vehicle for artists and music enthusiasts alike."

Shortly afterward, there was a vacation period. Hetfield embarked on a bear hunting trip in Siberia. Hunting had always been high on James's list of recreational priorities, but this trip was more remote and solitary than anything he'd undertaken. In addition to hunting bears, James spent a lot of time holed up drinking vodka. During that period he missed the first birthday of his son, Castor.

The next time any news came out of the Metallica camp was in July. The band announced that all album activities, including recording, had ceased while Hetfield entered rehab to "undergo treatment for alcoholism and other addictions."

While the timing was surprising, the facts were not. Hetfield's drinking issues were well documented. What was more unnerving was the mention of "other addictions," and speculation was rife as to what they were. Newsted quickly dismissed any suggestion that James had drugs issues. It said a lot about Hetfield's growth that he was willing to address those issues; quitting drinking would benefit both his personal and business life. After all, he had always made clear that family was number one.

The response to the news was generally positive, and messages of support flooded in from friends and peers across the music industry. There were dozens of people who were happy to come forward as admirers of the man.

A short time into the rehab period, a message from James appeared on the Metallica website: "It took a lot for me to admit to my problems, and it's a great feeling to have the support and comfort for me as a person from all the friends I've made out there. Thanks very much, it means a lot."

Little else was heard from Hetfield for several months, until another message appeared on the website: "Yes, folks, we have word from James, and the news is all good. His recovery has gone exceedingly well; he is back out, about and feeling good about life." This was good news, and Hetfield added his own message: "My music and lyrics have always been therapy for me. Without this God-given gift, I don't know where I'd be."

We know from the *Some Kind of Monster* documentary—for which initial filming had begun in the spring of 2001, prior to Hetfield entering rehab—that during Hetfield's time in rehab, his bandmates wondered if he would ever return to Metallica. Ulrich found this especially hard to take. The idea of Hetfield not returning led Ulrich to suggest that Hetfield controlled when he was present and controlled when he was absent.

The rehab period was as good a time to regroup for the others as it was for James. Simply put, James Hetfield is the beating heart of Metallica. Considering it was possible that he'd never return to the band, there must have been a few anxious faces in the larger Metallica camp as the weeks became months in 2001.

Hetfield emerged from rehab on February 19, 2002, seemingly a reformed man. While he had been away, his wife, Francesca, had given birth to their third child, Marcella, on January 17. The prospect of another child must have been a huge incentive to triumph during intensive rehab.

When the news broke about James's recovery, there was relief on all fronts—and intrigue as to which James would return. Prior to his hiatus, the band had received counseling from a life coach named Dr. Phil Towle, who was better known for dealing with large sports franchises.

Towle's role was to improve communication and understanding between high-profile, high-earning individuals. While Metallica had lost the ability to communicate effectively and that had influenced their creative output, many observers were concerned that a rock band would undertake such extreme "therapy." Newsted thought that the approach was overkill, and in an interview for *Some Kind of Monster*, he described it as "fucking lame . . . weak."

A brief appearance at MTV's *Icon*, for Hetfield's heroes Aerosmith, was James's first venture onstage since rehab. He recalled, "This is the first time I have been on a stage since I came out of rehab, so I'm a little nervous. My heart is pounding fast, so let me know if I am talking too fast."

This was touching display from Hetfield was worlds away from the overconfidence most people exhibit while fueled by alcohol. For those looking for a more relaxed Hetfield, the signs were good. Newsted gave a positive report following his first postrehab meeting with James. "He's a changed man," said Newsted. "It was good . . . we're brothers, man."

2002 continued with little news of either new material or who was going to play bass on the new record. What seemed most likely was that Rock would fill in on bass duties, at least until a suitable replacement for Newsted could be found. The band moved and recorded at their own studio space, which was referred to as HQ. That process began in earnest on April 12, 2002.

The process of recording an album had changed a great deal since Metallica's last time in the stu dio. James was only willing to commit certain hours (11:00 am to 4:00 pm) each day to work activities—a sensible approach given his recovery. For Ulrich, such a specific time frame was a serious problem, especially given his notorious preference for being nocturnal. There was a huge conflict from the start.

The informal agreement was that there should be more equal contribution from all band members—with all three taking an equal hand in writing music and lyrical ideas. Hetfield's daily curfew meant that the situation did not always work out well.

Very little was known about the music the band was working on. What had come out was that it wouldn't be a polished affair, instead using rawness and spontaneity to reflect the various moods at the time. It was even suggested that the band would be revisiting the sound of their early material.

One theme that kept coming up was anger, and as 2002 rolled into 2003, nobody outside of the band had any clue as to what this new material would sound like. That confusion wasn't exactly helped by Hammett's mentioning of Swedish band Meshuggah as a possible comparison either. Matters were made worse when Ulrich added Hatebreed and Entombed to that list of influences. In retrospect, a combination of any of the above would have been welcome.

What helped the band turn the corner was the announcement of Rob Trujillo as the band's new bass player. He had been plying his very able trade with Ozzy Osbourne's band and, prior to that, with hardcore/metal act Suicidal Tendencies. Footage of Trujillo being offered the role showed Metallica stressing that he was a band *member*, not a hired musician. You couldn't help but admire the open way in which Hetfield, Ulrich and Hammett welcomed him into the fold.

The band was seemingly astounded by how easily Trujillo delivered the Metallica basslines he'd been asked to learn. All who saw his first rehearsal agreed he was the man for the job. Trujillo was a quiet and extremely polite individual. Unfortunately for Trujillo, he arrived too late to play on the new album. Those bass parts had already been handled by Rock.

Hetfield recognized that his controlling habits were not a positive force. "Lars and me came into the studio and told the others what to do," Hetfield admitted. "Everything had to be under my control. Totally childish."

A picture was building regarding the likely sound of the new record, which was to be called *St. Anger*—a concept loosely based on the St. Christopher pendant that many people wear for good luck. Rock—a master of polished, commercially appealing rock records—gave an interview with *Metal Hammer* and seemed liberated by the no-rules approach they had taken in the studio. "We wanted a raw, unpolished sound," Rock admitted. "We played it all live without overdubs. . . . For example I only needed ten minutes for the drum sound."

On the surface, all of that sounded promising. But given all that had gone on in the Metallica camp in recent years, there was a sense of apprehension. The buildup to the release continued at pace during the spring of 2003, with the band recording a video for the first single (the title track) at the infamously tough San Quentin prison in San Francisco. Metallica had another duty to perform, too, and that was to head to LA for the MTV *Icon* show, which would honor them that year. It was a strange night—particularly for Trujillo—involving several mainstream acts (including Avril Lavigne) doing their own take on a few Metallica tracks. It was a meaningful tribute from MTV, especially given that Metallica were hardly "their kind of band" for much of their career. If nothing else, the event offered some healthy publicity for the new record.

With Metallica's customary frenzied media machine firmly in motion, the album was released on June 5, 2003. This was five days in advance of the planned release date, out of fear that there'd be a premature leak on the Internet.

CHAPTER 14

THE WELL IS DRY

Fans who were uncomfortable with Metallica's post–"The Black Album" output were optimistic about *St. Anger*.

From the very first seconds of lead track "Frantic," it is obvious that there were issues with the general sound of the recording—despite the song being one of the better tracks on the album. The snare drum sound was certainly unusual in terms of how loose it sounded.

The rhythm guitar assault that had been so potent on early Metallica albums now seemed to carry far less threat. On closer, technical inspection, Hetfield was playing single, more resonant power chords as opposed to fast, technical riffing—with the only speed in each song coming from Ulrich's often grating snare drum sound.

During the process of recording *St. Anger*, Hetfield made several references to the fact that the lyrics and sound were influenced by the difficulties of the previous months. In fact, some consider the lyrics on the album to be among the band's least insightful.

"Rarely have I seen such an error of judgement by a band. The way that *St. Anger* was written, recorded and performed was 100% wrong," rock writer Joel McIver reckoned. "I understand the mechanics of recovery," McIver acknowledged, "but addiction is neither expressed or resolved with songs like 'Invisible Kid,' which are dross of the highest order."

The reception to *St. Anger* was mixed at best, although predictably, it occupied the top spot on the *Billboard* chart. For many critics, *St. Anger* was too much to take. Even the cover art seemed unimaginative, featuring a tightly restrained fist on a cartoon orange background. While Malcolm Dome wasn't impressed, he qualified his criticism: "*St. Anger* was an awful album for sure, but at least it was *their* awful album. By that I mean it wasn't a compromise of any kind and was a statement of where the band was at that time."

Hugh Tanner, who'd spent years looking in on Hetfield's career as a friend and a fan, had a balanced view of what it represented for all involved. "In many ways, it was a raw record they had to make, in order to bring to an end a raw period in the individuals involved's lives."

While there is truth to the above comments, more critical commentators viewed the record's supposedly angry nature as a façade for a desperate lack of ideas and direction. The mainstream press were confused but were hesitant to completely trash what many believed to be an honestly delivered statement on where the band stood emotionally. The garage-like sound was flagged up almost across the board, although the lack of coherent song structures was attributed—at least in some reviews—to Metallica going "back to basics."

Amazingly for an album that was supposedly an open forum for all members of the band, there were no guitar solos, which even Kirk Hammett had to try to justify. Apparently, it was an attempt to do what wasn't expected. In many people's eyes, *St. Anger* was a move away from the strengths of the band and an anomaly in their largely strong back catalog.

Regardless of the lukewarm reception that met *St. Anger*, Metallica rolled its huge production out on a summer tour with Limp Bizkit, Linkin Park and the Deftones— drawing vast audiences all over the country.

Metallica announced that the aforementioned *Some Kind of Monster* would be released. The movie was not a polished, feel-good exercise designed to extract more money from fans. It was a raw, documentary-style piece, covering the entire *St. Anger* process from Newsted's departure through to album release. Also included were interviews with the band while James went into rehab, discussions with therapist Dr. Phil Towle, and chats with other members of the Metallica "family."

Achieving all that required being highly intrusive, which fell to talented filmmakers Joe Berlinger and Bruce Sinofsky. They were skilled in the art of raw documentaries and had approached the band years earlier with the idea, only to be told that Metallica were not ready to bare all. Despite their track record with honest, cutting-edge filmmaking, nothing could have prepared them for the drama of the Metallica monster.

Berlinger was keen to identify the thrust of the film: "On the surface it's about the making of *St. Anger*, but it's much more a film about human relationships and the creative process." The relationship that was most scrutinized was the one between Hetfield and Ulrich. While the two thought they had been communicating adequately over the years, the reality was somewhat different. Much like many marriages and other close relationships, too many assumptions were made, gradually forming a chasm of misunderstanding.

Ulrich openly admitted to not knowing his colleague at all, and some of the documentary's scenes depicted palpable levels of tension between the two. It was compelling viewing and far more interesting than any reality TV show, with some added spice coming from an interview with former band member Dave Mustaine. The key to the issue was that Mustaine felt disrespected because of what happened all those years ago in New York. He felt that the whole issue could have been handled differently and that if Hetfield had sought help with his drinking back then, the problem could have been averted.

Towle, whose role was to identify key issues from the band's past, saw the Mustaine saga as one that needed resolving. Mustaine came to San Francisco and was given the opportunity to talk one-on-one with Ulrich—the main focus of his irritation over the years. While the painful conversation with Ulrich unfolded, Mustaine looked drained. Ulrich, on the other hand, seemed sheepish about talking about the past. While mildly apologetic about it, he seemed surprised by how hurt Mustaine was.

The one person missing from that conversation was Hetfield—as Mustaine pointed out—and no closure was going to come. Hetfield distanced himself from the whole Mustaine debate over the preceding years, preferring to keep quiet about the matter. Anytime he was pressed, he took a diplomatic stance and avoided disrespecting

Mustaine. Despite the attention it got, the Mustaine issue was not the focus of the documentary. The main purpose was to reestablish a connection between the current band members, while revealing the true personalities of Hetfield, Ulrich and Hammett to the fans.

Berlinger explained, "James views it as something which allows him to communicate with the fans, to let them know who he really is. It shows his whole psychological mission . . . he could no longer pretend he was James Hetfield the front man offstage and on." Berlinger was right, although it's debatable whether the film illustrated why James went into rehab.

Some Kind of Monster was a huge turning point for Metallica as a band. Because it was so honest—uncomfortably so at times—it cleared away all the myths and bullshit that had accrued over the years, giving the band a clean slate both professionally and personally. Metallica fans flocked to see the movie, which aired in theaters worldwide in mid-2004, but it wasn't a huge commercial success.

The band were on tour at the time, having paused briefly to collect a Grammy award for *St. Anger* in the Best Metal Performance category. "The Unnamed Feeling" surfaced as a single, making it the third off the album, after "St. Anger" and "Frantic." Sales of the album were poor by the band's standards.

The live Metallica experience continued to impress—which was always the case even in troubled times. "During those so-called faltering times, every single live performance was beyond un-faltering," Eric Braverman protested. "Every one of those shows on that *St. Anger* tour, James Hetfield delivered the shit. It's the albums that have been the problem, never the live show."

While Hetfield continued to deliver compelling live shows, a few people noticed that he was a different person after rehab. Anthrax's Charlie Benante was one of them. Benante said, "I hadn't seen them for a while, but we ended up playing together in Germany while Metallica were promoting *St. Anger*. I had the most down-to-earth conversation I had ever had with James on that trip. I had gone through some stuff during the years prior to that where I was having these anxiety attacks. As a result I had to stop drinking . . . and in fact taking any stimulant. I had a bit of an awakening about things and we talked about that. He talked to me about what he went through and it was a very emotional talk. After that I would get text messages from him sporadically, and we would communicate that way."

Benante knew Hetfield since the early days in New York, and although they had drifted apart occasionally, they were closer than they had ever been. In Benante's opinion, the reason was that James was finally comfortable in his own skin. "I guess after I watched that movie, I kind of understood a little more," Benante mused. "And I guess what he was saying to me all made sense now."

Lonn Friend had his own problems in 2004 and was blown away by any meetings he had with the reformed Hetfield during the Californian leg of the *St. Anger* tour. "We had infrequent but always warm visits over the years, most significantly around the time of the Metallica shows in November 2004," Friend recalled fondly. "The band had just emerged from their *Some Kind of Monster* season in hell, but I was going through a divorce while living in the desert writing my book. James understood and offered consoling words. It was a moment between semi-kindred spirits."

In the wake of frenetic touring, the release of the *Some Kind of Monster* EP and exhaustion, Metallica returned to San Francisco for Christmas 2004. They were emotionally drained by the rigors of live shows and the aftermath of the *Some Kind of Monster* experience.

While they were on the road, they jammed on new material, and it seemed the results of those sessions would surface in the near future. Thanks to a fresh dynamic with Trujillo, Metallica had negotiated the hardest times of their career. While the music had suffered, the positives of a newfound respect for each other ensured a solid future.

For James Hetfield it was the beginning of a new life, and it wouldn't be overstating things to describe the rehab experience as his rebirth. He viewed things through different eyes, and on a personal level that was a huge step forward. For the first time in his career, he felt he was able to just be James Hetfield, with nothing to prove to himself or anyone else. What that meant for his music and the trajectory of Metallica remained to be seen. Without the experiences of the previous four years, it's possible that Metallica would not have been a functioning band.

CHAPTER 15

MAN IN THE BOX

By the end of 2004, it was rumored that Metallica had assembled many hours of riff ideas, song fragments and bass lines. It seemed as if the fog of the preceding years had lifted, and for James Hetfield personally, this was certainly a new dawn. What proved interesting was the question of whether the new Metallica—with a sober Hetfield—could summon the kind of aggression and creativity that their fan base wanted.

There was little doubt that their self-analysis had taken a heavy toll, and combined with the usual punishing touring schedule, it would have been no surprise if the band had disappeared for much longer than they did.

Hetfield had announced during a radio interview in 2004 that the band planned to begin working on new material during the spring of 2005. Nothing came of that suggestion in public, and 2005 was a quiet year on most fronts, with the exception of a Grammy nomination for *Some Kind of Monster* in the Best Hard Rock Performance category.

There was one significant announcement that year: Metallica parted ways with producer Bob Rock. Although they had no plans as to who would produce future material, the band felt that the relationship with Rock had reached its natural conclusion.

"As grateful as we are for all Bob has done for us since 1991, we feel it's time to move on," Lars Ulrich said in a press release. Hetfield threw in his own comments: "We've been thinking about this for some time now, it's just the way things have panned out."

The band members did their own thing, with Kirk Hammett taking some time off to perform with the FLUX string quartet. For James Hetfield, this was family time, and that was something he relished. The band did get together in September to record their voices for the *Simpsons*. November 2005 saw the band's only live shows of the year, and they didn't have to travel far. SBC Park in San Francisco was the venue for two concerts in the middle of the month.

An announcement in early 2006 confirmed that new material wasn't imminent. In March 2006 Ulrich announced that the band planned to dedicate the next six months to a new album. While they were doing so, Metallica had other commitments, including inducting Black Sabbath into the Rock & Roll Hall of Fame in March. It was a stirring event by any standards and featured respectful speeches from both Lars and James, as well as Metallica renditions of Sabbath classics "Hole in the Sky" and "Iron Man."

Metallica had touring commitments that year, which involved three shows in South Africa before they returned to Europe for the summer festival route. Metallica headed to the Far East for end-of-summer gigs in Japan (where new material was released) and South

Korea. Commercially, it was a quiet period, with only an acoustic set from the Bridge School Benefit in 1997 and a DVD of all the band's videos to date seeing the light of day in 2006.

It wasn't until early 2007 that Metallica gave any clear signs that new material was on their immediate agenda. Hammett had mentioned that the band had fifteen or so songs ready to move to the next stage. Hetfield commented on the relaxed attitude in the studio.

Several things had changed, however. First, the writing process was largely carried out at Metallica HQ, which had become a safe haven since the days of *Some Kind of Monster*. Second, they had a new producer, Rick Rubin, a guy whose working style was a million miles away from those of Bob Rock and Flemming Rasmussen. Whereas those two preferred close day-to-day involvement, Rubin's style was more detached—with fewer visits to the studio to listen to progress.

"Rick Rubin wanted us to focus on the essence of Metallica," Hetfield told MTV. "His essence was around *Master of Puppets*. He was trying to get us to think, *What were we thinking back then? What were we doing? What were we feeling? What were we influenced by?* Yes, it's interesting homework, but it's impossible to go backwards. We're evolvers; we like moving forward."

Hetfield was correct, of course. It would be pointless to recreate a mood whose origins lay twenty years in the past. But the fact that Rubin made the band *think* while keeping his creative distance seemed to be the refreshing tonic that Hetfield needed.

While Rock's brilliant input had worked, the new atmosphere in the studio went well. Hetfield noted that Rubin's style suited him and took some pressure off.

In this favorable environment, there was every opportunity for Hetfield and Metallica to come up with their best possible work. Rubin's regime was different in another way, too. In his world, Metallica would go nowhere near a recording studio until all the songs in question were as close to complete as possible. In the past the band had entered the studio with the songs as little more than demos.

On March 14, armed with the songs that were being considered for the new album, Metallica and their recording crew left HQ for Sound City Studios in Van Nuys, Los Angeles. This was the first time Metallica had recorded outside the Bay Area since 1991's "The Black Album." Sound City—was famous for being the birthplace of Nirvana's seminal *Nevermind,* among many other albums.

There was a possibility of returning to some longer, more complex songs, which was welcome news for older fans. New material had been played—in incomplete form—at shows in Berlin and Tokyo. However, Trujillo revealed that of the two new songs released, only segments of them would end up on the album.

During the summer of 2007, Metallica had several touring commitments, including the Live Earth concert on July 7 and a concert at Wembley Stadium in London the following day. While dedicating themselves fully to the live shows, the new record was their top priority.

In an interview with *Rock Hard,* Trujillo commented on how the album might sound: "I would say that this album is dynamic, heavy, groovin' and you'll probably be excited to know that there will be guitar solos on it! In addition, Lars remembered to tune his snare drum properly this time!"

In a television interview with NTV, Hetfield explained what the new record represented to him. "It's like opening a new chapter of a book," he said. "*St. Anger* was a cleansing of all our issues from the past. *Death Magnetic* feels new, feels fresh. New bass player, new producer, new attitude in the band, new gratitude in the band. So there is really a new feel."

Hetfield was a more amenable interviewee than previously, and Trujillo was clearly settling in well in order to offer such amusing responses. The fact that he'd bedded in so impressively on a musical level must have boosted his confidence. Trujillo was exactly the kind of upbeat, humorous guy that Metallica needed, and the fact that he could play brilliantly was a huge bonus.

"Robert is the best possible guy they could have on board, and it might well be that he is instrumental for making the band function better," said Eric Braverman, who knew Trujillo personally.

Instead of documenting this album as they had with *St. Anger*, Metallica offered fans insight into their progress via the official Metallica website. "Mission: Metallica" shared footage from the studio. Fans were given small tastes of how the music sounded, and on May 22, the band announced that the recording of *Death Magnetic* was complete. With Rick Rubin's job done, all that remained was for engineer Greg Fidelman to mix the album.

Metallica geared up for the *Death Magnetic* tour by appearing on that year's Ozzfest bill. This touring package had been around since 1996, and each year the interest in it had increased, to the point that it had become a significant event on the summer schedule. Shadows Fall, originally formed in Springfield, Massachusetts, in 1995, were one of the bands who filled the support slots on Ozzfest 2008. "We were lucky enough to play with them when they headlined," Shadows Fall's singer, Brian Fair, recalled. "They did a little barbecue afterwards, and they were cool enough to let all the opening bands watch them sound-check. Fair was impressed with Hetfield's attitude and hospitality, as he explained: "Some bands pull all that ego shit and clear you away when they are sound-checking. But here's the biggest fuckin' metal band on the planet and they are throwing everyone a barbecue."

Metallica did some shows at unlikely locations. One took place at Pima County Fairgrounds near Tucson, Arizona, on May 16.

"This thing was almost all the way into Mexico, and they were doing a low-key, or so they thought, show, for a radio station that does not play Metallica. Thirty thousand people showed up out of nowhere in the desert," Braverman recalled. "[People] were climbing fuckin' lampposts to see this show."

Braverman continued, "That day, James came right up to me and said, 'Hey, Arizona guy, how are you doing?' I was with one of my best friends who had his son with him, and James signed all his stuff, [playfully] hit me on the head and walked off wearing a Cliff Burton tribute T-shirt." Hetfield was friendly that day, and when the show started, that amiable side continued. Braverman said, "When I watched the show, I sat on the stage with them, and he was making funny faces at me and shit. It was insane."

While Metallica were on tour, Fidelman mixed the album. Fidelman's résumé was impressive, with engineering credits on albums by Johnny Cash, U2, Slipknot and Audioslave. Regardless of his experience, mixing a Metallica album was one of his most high-profile assignments to date, and he *had* to get it right—particularly given the disappointment with *St. Anger* in some circles.

As the September release date neared, Metallica headed to the desert outside Los Angeles to record the video for the lead single, "The Day That Never Comes." Shortly afterwards, it was announced on the Metallica website that *Death Magnetic* was mixed and mastered, and on September 1, the video for "The Day That Never Comes" debuted on Metallica.com. Eight days later, Metallica's eighth studio album—comprising ten tracks—was unleashed on the waiting world.

The cover art that adorned the various *Death Magnetic* "experiences" (the record was available in several different formats) looked like a submerged coffin. The inspiration for the title was apparently a photograph of the late Alice in Chains singer Layne Staley. Seemingly, Hetfield saw the album as a tribute to what he called rock 'n' roll martyrs.

"Thinking about death," Hetfield told KTV, "some people are drawn towards it—just like a magnet. Other people push [it away]. Also the concept that we're all gonna die sometimes is over-talked about and then a lot of times never talked about—no one wants to bring it up; it's the big white elephant in the living room. But we all have to deal with it at some point."

Had James's introspection made him think differently about life and death? Rex Brown thought so: "We got close during the time when we were on tour together, we'd text back and forth. James is a very knowledgeable, down-to-earth person. If you take care of mind, body and soul, everything is okay. After you've been through all the stuff that rock 'n' roll throws at you, there comes a point where you look and say, 'Thank you.'"

With a title related to death, it is rather appropriate that the album begin with a sound synonymous with life. Creeping in with the barely audible sound of a heartbeat, "That Was Just Your Life" is *Death Magnetic*'s first track. A clean, sinister intro, mildly reminiscent of "Enter Sandman" leads straight into a satisfyingly powerful guitar salvo of considerable power and authority.

If *Death Magnetic* is anything to go by, Hetfield's rehab period had helped his creativity, and for many, his lyrics and songwriting were near top form. Hetfield seemed to have rediscovered some of the lyrical bite that had been missing in the mid-1990s output. The mainstream press widely praised the record, and more than a few suggested that it was a return to greatness for the band. *Death Magnetic* was not a return to old school thrash, but for many fans it was a significant improvement on everything since 1991.

Not everyone agreed. Malcolm Dome had his own view: "In some ways *Death Magnetic* was the band compromising for the first time in their career. It was almost as if they had said, 'What do people want from us?' rather than them saying, 'This is who we are, this is what we are, this is what we're giving you, make your own mind up.' I don't like the album at all, and I don't think it's really *their* album."

Many critics and listeners suggested the sound was suffering from an overly compressed dynamic range in an attempt to increase volume. This resulted in too much distortion. There was something strange about *Death Magnetic*'s sound, which was hardly a new issue for a Metallica album. Q Prime were keen to bury the matter, and Cliff Burnstein and later Lars Ulrich both said that they were happy with the final product.

Most people seemed happy with *Death Magnetic* and were impressed with Hetfield's contribution to an album that bore his lyrical and musical imprint. *The Guardian* declared, "[It's] the strongest material the band have written in twenty years." The UK's *Uncut* magazine was similarly pleased, saying, "Like all the best heavy rock albums, it suspends your disbelief, demands your attention and connects directly with your inner adolescent."

Straight after the release, the band headed on the road with important shows in Europe, most notably a Metallica fan-club event at London's O2 Arena on September 15. There would be no letup, as ahead lay a comprehensive US tour beginning in Glendale, Arizona, on October 21.

David Ellefson went to a show and caught up with James backstage. He recalled, "I had a great conversation with James. It was really good. We've got families and we've been through some things in our lives. Sometimes we find common ground as gentlemen, because our lives are much richer with experience now."

Ellefson was raised with a strict Christian background, and after struggling with some of the usual excesses that the rock world can present, he returned to a more disciplined Christian way of thinking. Ellefson said, "I'm always happy to see other people succeeding when they go through a transition, and when I saw him I thought, 'He's got it, man. He's got the spirit—he's got the fire in him.' He was glowing like a golden angel and I'll never forget it. I was sitting there thinking, as big as this is—20,000 people all wearing Metallica shirts—I really got an impression that there is something even bigger for James than Metallica, or even life after Metallica, kind of in the same way that Bono is. [Bono] has really got into the Holy Spirit and he exudes something far beyond U2, as big as rock music is. I saw that in James, too, and my hope for him as a friend is that it continues. A lot of people struggle with these kinds of transitions, and it was nice to see that James was being successful in it."

Hetfield was in a good place and the band had sufficient warm-up shows to ensure that the new Metallica live experience was great for all concerned. World Magnetic—as the tour was called—was a little unusual because the support acts were changed at regular intervals, and that was no bad thing. For example, the first US shows in October and November featured the heavy super-group Down and prehistoric doom merchants Sword as guests. December saw Lamb of God stand in, with the exception of the two shows at the LA Forum, which had Machine Head on the bill. Down was an appropriate choice, not least because they included former Pantera bass player Rex Brown.

Brown recalled, "We got the first part of the World Magnetic Tour, which was really cool. James and I would talk every night about certain stuff—and it didn't always have to be about recovery. We bonded on a certain level."

Brown and Hetfield had similar views on a lot of life's challenges, and Brown felt strongly about public and media intrusion issues. Brown said, "Everybody knows that James is sober now, but it's really none of anyone's fuckin' business."

On December 2, World Magnetic swung into Vancouver. Canada had long been a hotbed of metal, and Annihilator would rank high on any fan's list of vital Canadian thrash outfits. Formed in 1984, Annihilator was founded in Ottawa, and their main man was a gifted guitar player by the name of Jeff Waters. To say that Waters had virtuoso guitar skills would be an understatement. But Annihilator didn't get the attention they deserved, despite some excellent albums in the 1980s, of which 1989's *Alice in Hell* is often considered to be the high-water mark.

Given that the two bands had similar timelines, you would have thought that Hetfield's and Waters's paths would have crossed earlier, particularly given their status as two of metal's best axe-men. The two had never met. "I was in Australia mixing a band," Waters explained. "I intentionally stopped over on the way to Vancouver to see the Metallica show. I had heard the new record and thought it had a vibe of the *...And Justice for All* era, and it was something I couldn't miss—to see them again."

Waters's means of access was Lamb of God's Willie Adler. Waters recalled, "I said to Willie, 'Any chance I can meet the guys?' And he says, 'Fuck yeah, you don't know them already?' I think I met Kirk first, and he said, 'Jeff! I thought you were from Ottawa?' And I'm looking at Kirk Hammett thinking, 'How the fuck did he know I was from Ottawa?'"

What Waters was forgetting, of course, was that although the bands had never met, a shrewd student of the guitar game like Hammett would be well aware of him and his band. "I didn't see Lars, and then James came in," Jeff continued. "And that was like meeting God. God just walked in the room, and I only ever had that feeling with Robert Plant before, maybe Angus Young. So there I am in a room with James Hetfield, the only guy I have ever got all shaky for, and Willie says, 'Go talk to him!' So I go over and say, 'Hi, my name is Jeff,' and I might have said, 'I'm a huge fan of yours' and that was the end of the conversation."

Waters continued, "I hadn't said my name was Jeff Waters, and that might have been a stupid mistake by me." Waters's chance was gone for now, but he redeemed himself later in Ottawa. Waters's story illustrates the huge aura that James Hetfield still commanded, and this was even the case for established rock musicians. Hetfield is truly an icon, and although his ways of dealing with fame have changed over the years, the effect he has on those around him is undiminished.

Touring continued through the end of 2008 before the band headed over to Europe. Before the European leg of the tour, though, James reconnected with another face from the early days in Downey: Jim Arnold. "Last year I was able to get in touch with him. I had not talked to him since 'The Black Album' tour at the LA Forum," Arnold recalled. "He left tickets and backstage passes for me and another old friend [James Ungeheier], so we got to meet with him (almost in private), just James Ungeheier, his daughter, my son and me. He talked to us for about forty-five minutes. It was very cool. I am amazed to see that after all his success that he is the same cool guy we used to hang out with back in the day. He doesn't seem to have changed a bit!"

"Looking back now," Arnold said, "I would say that James was someone who really pursued the rock star dream. He dedicated all of his time to it, and out of all of the musician friends that we knew he seemed to be the most serious. I don't think any of us back then really expected him, or anyone else we knew, to make it big."

With Machine Head and Sword as backup, Metallica took arenas by storm. A refreshing feature of the tour was the vastly changing setlist. "I used to be able to predict when James Hetfield would burp onstage," Braverman reckoned. "Now I don't even know what songs they are going to play. It wasn't only that, though."

For years, James Hetfield had taken pleasure in the gratuitous and humorous use of expletives between numbers. "I remember shows where James would stand there and just see how many swear words he could run together consecutively. Just for the hell of it," Braverman recalled. "Instead of [swearing], now there are beach balls. The irony is, in the days when he did cuss all the time, Metallica would deliver a cookie-cutter set, playing the same fifteen songs as every other night."

As Braverman pointed out, the modern Metallica show had a more family-friendly vibe. Hetfield only used polite—and at times motivational—wording when engaging with the fans. While an indication of his growth since rehab, Hetfield's new approach changed the feel of a Metallica show.

At the end of every World Magnetic show, Metallica logo beach balls were released onto the stage from a net high above, allowing the band to goof around while playing their final encore song, which was usually "Seek and Destroy." It was all great fun, but it wasn't something you could imagine Hetfield doing if you had seen him stripped to the waist and in a Jagermeister-induced haze back in the mid-1980s. But things had changed. That was over twenty years ago.

This represented two things. First, there was greater emphasis on making rock concerts—and, for that matter, society as a whole—more family-friendly in recent years. Second, Metallica had become a huge corporate beast, so *everything* was branded, even the oversized Metallica beach balls.

Family was much more important in Hetfield's personal life, which was likely carried forward into his professional life, too. "I saw James at one of the first shows after his rehab and he looked very robotic and very tentative," old friend John Kornarens recalled. "As time went on, he's gotten better. I saw them last year and he looked totally confident—he looked great. I was happy for him because I've known him a long time, and now he has kids. I hope he finds some real balance. He has everything he could ever want moneywise. I think he's in a great spot nowadays, and somehow he has survived."

Hetfield had survived, and his obvious confidence and happy demeanor during these World Magnetic shows were very encouraging signs. The tour rolled on through the East Coast and the Midwest during January, and in February the awards came pouring in for *Death Magnetic* at the Grammys.

A slew of prestigious awards came their way, including Best Recording Package for the album, Best Metal Performance for "My Apocalypse," Best Rock Instrumental for "Suicide and Redemption," Best Rock Album for *Death Magnetic*, and Best Producer for Rick Rubin.

It was announced that Metallica were to be inducted into the Rock & Roll Hall of Fame in 2009, with a ceremony scheduled for April 4, in Cleveland, Ohio. While that was huge news and was certainly deserved, when the day came around, it was particularly meaningful in the life and career of James Hetfield.

Before any of this happened, the band had some important European dates to fulfill, including two shows at the O2 Arena in London in March. The vastly different set lists drew material from the band's entire back catalog. The *Death Magnetic* material got a thorough airing, with some weaker album moments like "Cyanide" translating well to the live arena. Unexpected tracks like "Fight Fire with Fire" and "Outlaw Torn" provided interesting variation, to the point that the Metallica live experience had become compelling rather than pre-dictable. The tour broke for much of April, and the band prepared for what was sure to be an emotional day in Cleveland, with several ghosts of the past ripe for exorcism.

CHAPTER 16
FRIENDS AGAIN?

Being inducted into the Rock & Roll Hall of Fame were the current band members, along with Jason Newsted and the late Cliff Burton. Hetfield invited pretty much everyone who had been involved with the history of Metallica. Everyone was flown in at the band's expense and accommodated in top hotels. It was an unprecedented display of friendship from Metallica. "I saw James at the Rock & Roll Hall of Fame and it was a great trip. They flew us all in for the show," Lloyd Grant recalled.

"He invited me to Cleveland, and that was very cool," Ron McGovney said. "I hadn't hooked up with James for a few years and I noticed a difference. The most significant thing about him was that he is very confident about himself now. He was very shy all these years ago. He absolutely grabs the attention of everyone who is in the same room with him now. Not just that, he later invited me and my kids to the shows at Charlotte and Atlanta, and James went out of his way to make my kids' first concert experience one that they will never, ever forget."

While McGovney was not inducted (he had never played on an album), the invitation was a belated but generous acknowledgement of all his work and dedication to Metallica in those formative days. The Cleveland trip was a joyous gathering of many people from Metallica's past, and the mood was one of mutual appreciation, respect and gratitude. Lonn Friend recalled, "The band performed the unprecedented act of flying people in from all over the world—close to two hundred of them—who were part of their journey from the Bay Area garages to global domination. James was sober and friendly, shaking hands and exchanging words with every guest who attended—me included."

The ceremony featured emotionally charged acceptance speeches from all the inductees and an upbeat speech from Burton's father, Ray. It was appropriate that at a ceremony involving no less than three bass players, the induction was done by Flea from the Red Hot Chili Peppers.

Jason Newsted's presence was particularly special, and his speech was emotional too. He concluded with that timeless acknowledgement to Metallica's millions of fans worldwide: "Without you, there could be no us." It hit home while Newsted fought back tears.

Hetfield was calm and very assured behind the microphone. Exuding an amazing level of positivity, James was a revelation. As David Ellefson alluded to previously, he looked and behaved as if he were operating on an almost ethereal level. "I'd like to give some huge gratitude to my higher power. For the gift of music and the awareness of my destiny early on," Hetfield said. "Music is my therapy, and I need to do it. I would love to thank my wife, Francesca, for saving my life

. . . many times. My children, all three of you are here. Thank you for teaching me how to love."

Despite the highly charged emotional content, Hetfield's demeanor was the culmination of a lifetime of hurt, hard work and success. "This is living proof," Hetfield roared while pounding the podium, "that it is possible to make a dream come true."

Hetfield finished by thanking Lars Ulrich for calling him all those years ago and including him in his dream to form the biggest heavy metal band in the world. With that, he turned around and picked up the grinning Ulrich in a bear hug that you just knew was genuine, bringing the audience to its feet.

The actual musical performance was a bonus. Taking to the stage again, Newsted roared through renditions of "Enter Sandman" and "Master of Puppets," followed by an encore of Aerosmith's "Train Kept-A-Rollin" alongside Johnny Burnette & The Rock 'n' Roll Trio.

The Cleveland weekend was a momentous occasion for all concerned, and it was a turning point in that James seemed happy to reconnect with key people from his past. What followed in future months was a continuing commitment to reconnect with former friends and associates. As the World Magnetic extravaganza rolled on, several old faces were welcomed back. One was Michael Alago, with whom James had lost contact. Alago confirmed that it was great to reconnect with James when the band played at Madison Square Garden in New York: "I haven't really kept in touch with James, but I saw him backstage and thought he looked awesome . . . all grown up, of course, and now he seemed like a very focused man and performer." There was an effort made during World Magnetic to embrace many of the people who had become distant during Metallica's ascent into megastardom.

The band took World Magnetic back on the road to Europe and Mexico over the next few months. Touring ground on during the fall months, mostly through the East Coast, the Midwest and Canada. When the tour came to Ottawa, Jeff Waters got an opportunity to redeem himself. He recalled, "I talked to James about Michael Alago, but I didn't really get a chance to have much of a longer conversation with him."

As to James's demeanor after that Ottawa show, Waters said: "Kirk Hammett was almost hugging me; that's how warm and friendly he seemed. James seemed to be ten feet taller than he really is and just very guarded." Waters explained, "I'm making that assessment based on years of reading people. He's very much as if he has a wall up . . . when the wall comes down, they're normal guys and nice guys. But when you're as famous as James is, you have to have that wall there to protect yourself."

Waters's observation was correct, and the reason for it was simple, as he explained: "When you get to know people like James, I'm sure they are super-nice guys. But can you imagine the tens of millions of people who want to get to know that guy? It's a fuckin' corporation they are running, and they just can't let everyone in."

With the World Magnetic tour pausing in December, Metallica received another Grammy nomination for the following year's ceremony, when "Unforgiven III" won in the Best Hard Rock Performance category. With their year at an end, Metallica could reflect on their restored position in the larger metal tapestry.

While other acts appeared on the scene and threatened to take things to a much higher level, no band could match Metallica's crushing economic might. Forget that *Death Magnetic* was a fairly safe record by Metallica's standards. With staggering sales figures and an ascent to Number 1 in thirty-four countries, *Death Magnetic*'s job was already done. Metallica were back as the biggest band on the planet, and that situation didn't look like it would change so long as Metallica's will to be there remained.

The last word on that is best left to Rex Brown. "I stood in the same exact spot every night. Every time during 'For Whom the Bell Tolls,' James would come up and hit my hand," Rex said. "And all I am thinking is, '*This* is the band I met twenty-five years ago. They've sold fuckin' over 100 million records and I can't believe it . . . that they've come full-circle like this."

CHAPTER 17

BIG FOUR TOGETHER

The two years of touring behind *Death Magnetic* continued until November 2010—a long haul even by Metallica's road-loving standards. The tour reputedly grossed over $200 million in ticket receipts. It's easy to see why they kept the tour rolling. Prior to the final shows in Melbourne, Australia, in late November, an event took place that few thrash metal fans could have ever imagined.

The so-called Big Four—Metallica, Anthrax, Megadeth and Slayer—announced that they would share a concert stage in Warsaw, Poland, on June 16, 2010. Even though the four bands had been around since the mid-1980s and various permutations had appeared on bills together, this was the first time that all four of thrash metal's most seminal acts performed together. With their commercial dominance resoundingly confirmed, Metallica topped the bill.

From all reports, James Hetfield was a significant catalyst behind the event. According to Hetfield, Metallica's induction into the Rock

& Roll Hall of Fame was a learning process for dealing with former bandmates. This was particularly true with Dave Mustaine, whose invitation was a mature and compassionate olive branch on Hetfield's behalf. Now, the Big Four concept—with Mustaine seemingly happy to play second fiddle to his nemesis—was another step in that direction.

"The Hall of Fame had a lot to do with turning around and embracing the past," he told *SVT Direct* prior to a Big Four show in Gothenberg, Sweden, on July 5. "It was part of that vibe of maybe paying back for all the good things that have happened to us," he continued. "And also maybe helping some others along."

It seemed that the Big Four idea hinged on Hetfield and Metallica and that the motivation behind it was as much about boosting the profiles (and bank accounts, perhaps) of the other three bands as it was about Metallica. It would, after all, be big business.

A same-day broadcast of a Big Four show in Sofia, Bulgaria, on June 22 was screened in over 1,000 movie theaters worldwide, and the atmosphere was electric. A live Blu-ray and CD box set was released shortly afterwards, with different packaging offering posters, guitar picks and a color booklet. Several more Big Four shows followed in Europe, including a final gig in Istanbul, Turkey, on June 27.

2010 drew to a close on an emphatic note for Metallica and for heavy music in general. The massively successful Big Four shows in Europe (and the announcement that there would be more to follow on US soil in 2011) injected excitement into the metal scene. New recorded material was scheduled for release by three of the four bands (all but Slayer) in 2011. It would be interesting to see what effect this new sense of unity might have on the bands' respective creative processes.

For Metallica, that creative process took a wild turn, and for a band that had recorded an album as polarizing as *St. Anger*, that was really saying something.

The suggestion to collaborate with the legendary Lou Reed was apparently conceived as far back as Metallica's Hall of Fame induction in 2009, when Reed joined the band onstage to jam. According to Hetfield, Reed flippantly said—after being exaggeratedly animated about the experience of playing onstage with Metallica—that they should do a record together.

"'Yeah, right. Are you talking to us?' But he was serious," Hetfield recalled in an interview with *Rock and Pop FM* in Argentina. Hetfield's response at the time suggested that he wasn't taking Reed particularly seriously. It now seemed that *something* about what Reed had in mind was persuasive.

Originally it was suggested that Metallica would rerecord some of Reed's unreleased tracks, among which were a collection of demos composed for a play called *Lulu*. The play was based on two novels by German playwright Frank Wedekind about a wayward French prostitute. Upon reading the play's script and hearing the rough, accompanying demos, Metallica decided that *Lulu* had potential to be a full-blown collaboration. This was a side project that they all wanted to be involved with, although in the *Rock and Pop FM* interview, Hetfield said that it should not be considered a new Metallica album per se.

Before work on *Lulu* began in earnest (Reed wanted the band to record the tracks live in a studio), the Big Four series made its US debut at the Coachella festival in Indio, California, on April 23. While the European Big Four shows were a success, the anticipation for the first

US show was significantly ramped up—perhaps because the US, and California specifically, was considered one of the spiritual homes of thrash metal,

At an event that *felt* historic, an inspired Hetfield and Metallica owned the night. The fans—so amped by their heroes' performance and the aura of the day—built a makeshift bonfire in the center of the mosh pit. The final act of unity came in the form of a Hetfield-led encore featuring every member of all the bands, performing a rousing version of the Diamond Head classic "Am I Evil?" This showed that any rivalries and gripes would remain firmly in the past.

"We are looking to book something on the East Coast because of the success of this—it should hopefully come together in a week or two," Lars Ulrich said afterwards in an interview with *Rolling Stone*. "Maybe we'll do somewhere in the Midwest and South too. Still, I don't think it will turn into a 40-date arena tour; that would make it less special. I like the fact that there's an element of chaos to the whole thing. It shouldn't be sterile, streamlined and perfect: it needs an edgy underbelly to remain authentic."

The band took a break prior to returning to HQ in June, to work on the skeletal songs that Reed had been developing for the *Lulu* project. All the lyrics had already been developed by Reed, so what he needed was for Metallica to weigh in on the arrangement.

In attempting to sum up the narrative, Hetfield told Sirius XM's *Liquid Metal* that the focal character, Lulu, was "a siren who ends up being man's ruin. Everyone falls in love with her and she has no regard and no soul. She is soulless, out to party. She is doing what she wants and is out to break some hearts, but she is very captivating."

Hetfield said that the music would be "intense," and he was extremely complimentary about Reed's lyrics. "Every day there is a line I pull out and gnaw on it all day. It's not party rock, that's for sure," he declared.

Artistic collaboration between two disparate artists was not always smooth sailing. Ulrich admitted that at one point Reed—almost seventy years old at the time—challenged him to a street fight. Thankfully, as if to relieve the pressure, Metallica headed back to Europe for some more Big Four shows.

A second US show at New York's Yankee Stadium was booked for late September. Afterwards Hetfield told *Liquid Metal* about the future of the Big Four concerts: "Never say never, but it's run its course, in Europe and with the two shows on the coasts. It's done what it needs to do for now and we can go our separate ways, do our albums, do our things. Who knows what happens in the future? It could be the Big 10 eventually! There's no limitations. But this has been a blast. This might be the last one for at least a little while."

There was another foreign trip scheduled, with previously uncharted locales like Abu Dhabi, Delhi and Bangalore booked for shows. The Abu Dhabi show was particularly successful. Delhi promised to be a landmark event, but in the build up to the gig, some serious security issues came to light. The resulting show cancelation caused a near-riot. Security concerns were resolved sufficiently for the Bangalore show to take place in front of a rabidly enthusiastic audience, thus expanding the Metallica fan family even further.

A brief stop in San Francisco to shoot a video for *Lulu's* weird-sounding "The View" (with *Requiem for a Dream* and *Black Swan* director Darren

Aronofsky) preceded fleeting visits to London, Milan, Cologne and Paris for performances of mini live sets with Reed in support of *Lulu*.

So, what of *Lulu* itself?

Rolling Stone journalist David Fricke, who was fortunate enough to sit in on some of the recording process, boldly described what he heard as "a raging union of [Reed's] 1973 noir classic, *Berlin,* and Metallica's '86 crusher, *Master of Puppets.*" Was he being kind?

A cursory glance at online forums suggested that the fans thought so. *Lulu* eclipsed *St. Anger* as the most widely despised release of Metallica's entire catalog. Several songs were made available to stream on the Metallica and Lou Reed websites prior to the album's release on October 31. The first, "The View," received nasty comments online. In truth, the song did sound strange—almost as if Reed and Metallica were in separate rooms playing different songs. Reed's rambling lyrics over standard Metallica jamming made for an odd choice to represent the record.

Of the other songs, only "Pumping Blood," "Mistress Dread" and the rousing "Frustration" have anything in common with what we knew Metallica to be. Despite Hetfield's request for fans not to think of the music as a Metallica record and instead view it as a piece of stand-alone art, many critics slammed the idea for being too ambitious and a futile exercise in art for art's sake.

Time will tell, but *Lulu* will likely someday be acknowledged for what it was. It wasn't a Metallica album or a Lou Reed album but a free-styling collaboration between two important artists—people from entirely different worlds, not to mention two different generations. A classic? Possibly not, but by no means the abomination that many reviews called it.

The critical response was mixed at best. Reed admitted to being taken aback by some of the acerbic comments. He even claimed that some Metallica fans threatened to shoot him because of his part in the collaboration! *NME* magazine were positive, hailing *Lulu* as "a surprising triumph" and said that the record's "breadth and ambition is to be applauded. Metallica have performed way beyond what many thought them capable; they improvise freely as Reed's musical bitch, while for him this marks his most outré offering since *Metal Machine Music.*"

Other sources were far less complimentary, with *Pitchfork* tossing the record a rare 1.0 rating and dismissing its worth entirely: "For all the hilarity that ought to ensue here, *Lulu* is a frustratingly noble failure. Audacious to the extreme, but exhaustingly tedious as a result, its few interesting ideas are stretched out beyond the point of utility and pounded into submission."

Indicative of the sheer scale of criticism was the fact that Metallica rebutted some of it. Ulrich implied that he wasn't surprised by the reaction: "In 1984, when hardcore Metallica fans heard acoustic guitars on 'Fade to Black' there was a nuclear meltdown in the heavy metal community."

As always, Hetfield's tone was more reserved. He defended the record as Metallica "spreading their wings" and "trying something different."

Metallica ended a highly eventful year with another indication that they were comfortable with their past. They organized four 30th anniversary shows at San Francisco's Fillmore in early December. They were attended only by Metallica Club fans (who'd been invited to enter an August lottery to win tickets). The four shows sold out in a matter of minutes. In addition to players from other bands with which Metallica identified, the guest list included key characters from the band's past like Dave Mustaine, Jason Newsted, Ron McGovney, Hugh Tanner and Lloyd Grant, all of whom got up onstage and jammed at some point.

Mustaine joined the band onstage at the final show to play songs from *Kill 'Em All* and suggested afterward that Metallica wanted to make an album with him. Hetfield was fairly direct in an interview with the *So What?* fanzine, stating, "I see him healthier now. I see him as less of a bitter guy. But I do see a lot of stuff in the press with him talking about jamming with us and making an album. All this other crazy stuff? I read it and say to myself, 'Hold on. This is the Dave that we kind of wanted to forget about. You know, the big mouth that wants to just go-go-go.' But there *is* an authenticity about him when he speaks. He doesn't think too much before he does. He just goes off the cuff. Plus, when he says stuff like that, it's well-intended."

To coincide with the 30th anniversary concerts, Metallica released an iTunes-only EP entitled *Beyond Magnetic*. It consisted of four songs that hadn't made the final cut for *Death Magnetic*, although in some fans' eyes, at least two should have. "Hate Train," "Hell and Back," "Rebel of Babylon" and "Just a Bullet Away" were a strong quartet of songs. The EP went to the top of the download charts and prompted a release on CD on January 30, 2012.

The critical response was mainly positive, with *Artistdirect* saying the EP "sounds like an uncaged beast ready to once again rip rock 'n' roll a new one."

As if Metallica hadn't made enough big announcements in recent months, they added another to the list on February 7, airing plans for a festival called *Orion Music + More* on June 23 and 24 in Atlantic

City, New Jersey. They would headline both shows, playing their game-changing 1991 *Metallica* album in its entirety on one night and 1984's *Ride the Lightning* on the other.

At a press conference prior to the event, Hetfield explained why the band chose those two particular records: "*Ride the Lightning* started to splinter us off from your Slayers and other thrash bands. A song called 'Fade to Black' was an instant thorn in the side of the metal community. It was the first veering off the studded path. [The Black Album] became the album, I guess, that people needed to have. It's a gateway for people to get into Metallica."

Hetfield continued, "I would love it to be an annual thing and become an established festival that people can come to and know it's going to be good, no matter what. It'll be a fun place to be and hang and see some of the other things that are going to be happening, whether it's a car show or the movie tent that Lars is doing or Kirk's haunted mansion. . . . If it ends up staying in Atlantic City—who knows, it could move. It could end up being three days; it could just be one. It really depends on how it goes this time."

Ulrich hinted in the same interview that there would be no new Metallica album until at least early 2014. Whenever it appeared, it would not be released on Warner Brothers, as the band left the company in favor of creating their own independent record label, Blackened Recordings. Consistent with their longstanding desire to control their commercial destiny, they also acquired all master rights to their previous recordings.

"We would like to thank everyone at the Warner Music Group for 28 years of a fantastic relationship, particularly since 1994, where we truly felt we had partners in every aspect of our business in North America," said Hetfield in a press release.

Blackened Recordings was responsible for Metallica's audio and video material going forward. The company got straight to work with the release of a live concert DVD, *Quebec Magnetic*, from the World Magnetic Tour. Fans voted which songs should be included, and the remainder appeared as "extras." The DVD was released on December 11, 2012, and sold 14,000 copies in its first week, propelling it to Number 2 on the *Billboard* Top Music Videos chart.

A triumphant *Revolver* Golden Gods awards in May, where Hetfield shared the stage with Judas Priest's Rob Halford for a rousing version of "Rapid Fire," led into a successful second *Orion Music + More* festival in June. Thirty or so other bands joined Metallica for a breathless two days of activities.

Asked at a press conference why he had chosen Detroit, Hetfield offered up a humorous response: "We heard you needed the grass cut!" On a more serious note, he continued, "We hope this will be the new—and hopefully permanent—site." Hetfield added, "This site is amazing. We love it here!" Hetfield said that band members expected to lose money on the festival—at least in the short term—but were more focused on creating a viable, eclectic gathering for music fans with a "backyard BBQ" feel. More than 40,000 fans attended the two-day event.

Metallica Through the Never came out on September 27, 2013. It was a 3-D feature movie with a live concert in the middle. The concept was as ambitious as anything the band had ever done. Hetfield told *Artistdirect*, "It was difficult. There are really two movies in one here.

There's the narrative and the filmed footage of us live. It was tough to get both of those things on the same track. . . . We had to really let go of the control. It's not like: 'There's this concert footage with some narrative in it.' It's both, and they both have to give and take to make it work."

The movie's title referenced a song from *Metallica*, as Hetfield explained in the same interview, "Well, when we were naming the movie, it was similar to how we name songs or albums. We thought, 'What's this thing's nickname? What's it telling us?' Sometimes, there are song titles you write and they're intense. They *need* to have a song around them. Other times, you're just naming it. . . . *Through the Never* just fit that because there was no way of describing this movie. . . . We came up with a title that was just as vague as the movie could be."

Hetfield continued, "On the episode of *The Colbert Report* we did, there was a joke like, 'What is *Through the Never? Beyond the Sideways?*' He was making fun of it, which put me in stitches, man. It was like, 'What the hell does that mean?' For me, the song 'Through the Never' was about exploring man's mind and how limited we are. In a way, this movie maybe breaks through some boundaries."

Metallica Through the Never debuted to a positive reception at the Toronto International Film Festival. Reviews were good, with *Rotten Tomatoes* stating, "Imaginatively shot and edited, *Metallica Through the Never* is an electrifying, immersive concert film, though its fictional sequences are slightly less assured." *Rolling Stone* liked it, too, referring to it as "a full-throttle expression of rock 'n' roll anarchy."

With *Metallica Through the Never,* Hetfield and Metallica distanced themselves from every other band of their kind. They compared it to

Led Zeppelin's *The Song Remains the Same*, and in doing so they categorized themselves appropriately. Yes, Metallica could share the stage with bands at *Orion Music + More* festivals and even Anthrax, Megadeth and Slayer at the Big Four shows. But 2012 and 2013 illustrated further that Metallica were peerless within heavy music, as a promoter of a brand on a genuinely worldwide level. After all, there were very few places Metallica *hadn't* played a concert. As if to reduce that list further, it was announced that they would play a gig in Antarctica of all places, in a specially constructed dome, on December 8, 2013.

Prior to departing for Antarctica, Hetfield received plaudits for his dedication to the Little Kids Rock foundation, the nation's leading provider of music instruction and instruments for public schools, at the annual Rockin' the Bay benefit event on November 9. Upon accepting the Livin' the Dream Award, Hetfield described what the foundation meant to him. "I'm a firm believer in creative expression through music. It is important to have it available from a young age, which is why I support Little Kids Rock's mission to make music education accessible to children," said Hetfield. "I've seen how music changes people's lives for the better and I am honored to have a part in helping the organization enrich young lives through the lifelong gift of music education."

When December came around, the Antarctica concert—nicknamed *Freeze 'Em All*—was attended by only 120 fans. It should be noted that the song "Trapped Under Ice" from *Ride the Lightning* did *not* appear on the set list! Fans heard the music through headphones only, with no amplification or sound system whatsoever—a truly unique event that Hetfield referred to as "the most memorable concert in Metallica history." It was a perfect end to another successful year in the life of Hetfield and Metallica.

The subject of new, recorded music just wasn't going away. Having pushed dates back on more than one occasion—admittedly to accommodate a variety of other events and commitments—it seemed Metallica would deliver new music sometime in late 2016. That said, they were in the fortunate position—one they had created—of not being answerable or accountable to anyone but themselves (and that included their millions of fans, apparently). In an interview with *HuffPost Canada*, Hetfield explained where Metallica stood. "Writing music is somewhat important to us," Hetfield said. "We focus. Focus."

"Hopefully [we will return to the studio] soon," Hetfield said in an interview with *Oakland Press*. "I'm itchin'. We have tons of material to sift through. That takes a lot of time, because there's a lot of great stuff. I know we only need a few songs, but there's 800 riffs we're going through. It's kind of insane. We have sifted through a lot of the stuff and pulled the cream of the crop—it's just sitting there waiting for us to take it to the next level."

Asked why it had taken so long to start the process, Hetfield continued: "I know we do need to decompress after this, get this [*Metallica Through the Never*] film thing out of our systems. It's taken up a lot of time and a lot of effort. We go full-throttle into something and multitasking is not what we're after."

When presented in the same interview with the numbers ($2.72 million and counting) generated by *Metallica Through the Never*, Hetfield focused more on the act of creation than the commercial impact. "I didn't really have any huge expectations," Hetfield explained.

"I'm just excited to have the baby out of the womb and walking around now, finally, (after) two years at least with the process as it was—and having the idea for decades. As far as (box office) numbers coming back, management is certainly a little more focused on numbers and all of that and what it means. I don't know much about the movie world. As an artist, I just like that the thing is out there. It's exactly what we wanted, and we're proud of it."

Hetfield was as focused as ever on the creative aspect of his work. It's hard to imagine that money was a motivator, especially considering that Metallica was willing to make overtly noncommercial decisions in pursuit of creative satisfaction. If creative satisfaction coincided with commercial success (as it had more than it hadn't for Metallica), then so be it. But Metallica would not be the band they were if they weren't willing to challenge themselves—and fan loyalty—by throwing themselves into curveball projects like *St. Anger, Lulu* and—to a lesser degree—*Metallica Through the Never.*

With Hetfield in control just as he'd always been, with a far more mature and grounded outlook, it seemed certain that Metallica would continue pushing the envelope musically. In this world of burgeoning social media interaction, there would always be a new fan base waiting to discover them as long as they continued to create music. Consequently, the band/fan synergy would be preserved.

On August 18, 2016, Metallica announced that their new double-album, *Hardwired… to Self-Destruct,* would be released exactly two months later. Thus ending years of speculation and waiting.

Accompanying the announcement was the video for "Hardwired." In its breathless three minutes, the new song went a long way toward allaying any fears about Metallica's direction. With its snappy riffing and Hetfield's clipped vocal lines, it harkened back to the Metallica of the 1980s. It had a modern production polish and incorporated a warm, bass-rich sound that seemed far removed from *Death Magnetic*'s claustrophobic and overly compressed tone. The song was a definitive statement, and it worked—the reception was positive across the board. "Hardwired" was later nominated for the Grammy Award for Best Rock Song.

In mid-September, the band released a second track from the record, "Moth Into Flame." Anticipation for the new album swelled further. Albeit more than six minutes long, "Moth Into Flame" was a conceptually simple track that drew upon all of Metallica's influences dating back to the early 1980s, especially the New Wave of British Heavy Metal. Hetfield's improved singing was noticeable. Since the *Load* era, his vocals had been criticized for slipping into lazy, sonic hyperbole on the back of overly elongated vowels.

On Halloween, the band released "Atlas, Rise!"—an exciting amalgam of the *Kill 'Em All* era's tight chug and '90s Metallica's hard rock swagger. It seemed Hetfield and Metallica had rediscovered the fun of making music. While the fan base-appeasing *Death Magnetic*, seemed forced and overwrought in retrospect, the taster songs from *Hardwired... to Self-Destruct* showed a band free of constraints and comfortable with both their past and their present. Most Metallica fans were already satisfied that the band had recaptured something from their earlier years.

In an unusual move, as the release date approached, the band chose to drip-feed the other tracks and accompanying videos to the fans. Each song aired on a variety of websites worldwide, with the last released the day before the album dropped.

The response likely exceeded even the band's expectations. Despite the nearly eighty-minute running time, Metallica of 2016 was a lean beast. Gone was the overthinking that had plagued *Death Magnetic*. *Hardwired… to Self-Destruct* offers exhilarating aural snapshots of Metallica's thirty-plus–year career. Mid-tempo tracks like "Now That We're Dead" and "Here Comes Revenge" are nods to *Metallica*. The groovy "ManUNkind" is reminiscent of *Load*. Speedier cuts like "Hardwired" and "Spit Out the Bone" recall the angry youth of *Ride the Lightning*. In an interview on Italian radio with "Linea Rock," Hetfield discussed the diversity of the songs: "They're all great; I'm proud of every single one of them. It's a good mixture of variety of what Metallica does good."

First week sales confirmed the fervor for the band's creative rebirth. In addition to debuting at number one on the *Billboard* 200 chart, with sales of 291,000 units, the record hit the top spot in 57 other countries. The critics were kind, with *Rolling Stone* declaring that the record "Shreds back to vintage eighties terror." *Pop Matters* said, "More than anything, Metallica sounds like they're having fun again." Hetfield's vocal and guitar performances were singled out for praise in reviews.

Whatever *Hardwired… to Self-Destruct*'s legacy might be, the album redressed most, if not all, of the missteps Metallica had made in recent years. Metallica finally stepped out of their own shadow and caught up with themselves by making an album that not only honored their legacy but also ably represented fifty-plus-year–old men with little left to prove. It is a massively significant moment in their career.

CHAPTER 18

JUDGEMENT DAY

While it was a painful exercise for James Hetfield, *Some Kind of Monster* was the best way to make information available to the public. Without its stark honesty about Hetfield, all we would have had was speculation and rumors.

As human beings, we all encounter problems in life. Although Hetfield's are a matter of public interest because of who he is, they are no different from those of millions of human beings around the world. As stated at the start of this book, the environment a person grows up in can significantly influence every aspect of his or her life. Given that Hetfield had a tough start, it's a miracle that he became the man he did. As he has said, music has been his therapy, and that's the bottom line.

To fully appreciate what makes James's musical abilities so vital to rock music, we should concentrate on other musicians' testimony. Testament's Alex Skolnick, a talented musician within the parameters of heavy metal as well as a virtuoso in other styles of music, believes that James has a very special talent: "I'm convinced that had he chosen to play drums, bass or lead guitar in his band, James would have been just as influential and virtuosic." Skolnick definitely has a point, especially considering that at various points in his career, James fulfilled all of those roles.

Hugh Tanner agrees with Skolnick's suggestion, and having been present during those formative years in Brea, he's better qualified than most to comment. Tanner said, "James could sit at the piano and sound good and he could sit behind a drum kit and play. In fact, at that time . . . he would have been a better drummer than Lars."

Hetfield's destiny was with the guitar, and that's where the true depth of the man's musical ability lies. Whether it is his tight rhythm delivery or his loose and soulful lead work, Hetfield has it all. Skolnick said: "As a rhythm guitarist, he has had more of an impact on the guitar than most lead guitarists. A great lead guitarist himself, [his] occasional solos are among Metallica's most memorable, proving that speed and chops are secondary to melody." In a world where a guitarist's skill and worth are increasingly judged on outlandish technical wizardry, Skolnick's assessment of Hetfield's solid playing is even more apt.

Skolnick continued, "He is also a fine acoustic guitarist, playing intricate parts with a lot of depth, consistency and dynamics." Much of Hetfield's acoustic skill is probably borne out of endless hours on tour buses, with little access to amplified sound. His interest in country, blues and folk styles might have made this side of his guitar playing more polished.

Kreator's Mille Petrozza, widely considered the king of European thrash (and a singer and rhythm guitarist himself) shared Skolnick's opinion: "To be honest, I have lost track of them since 'The Black Album.' I still respect them for everything they've done, but for some reason I could never get into the country/rock/alternative touch they put into their music since the '90s. But despite feeling that way about the music, I still think that he is one of the best, if not *the* best, rhythm guitarist in all of metal."

Lonn Friend is one of the few nonband members to witness the riff-lord himself in the studio, having been present on a daily basis at "The Black Album" sessions. Friend said, "In modern hard rock history, no one stands any taller than James Hetfield. He defined the speed metal rhythm riff and transitioned what was once fodder for the underground into mainstream success."

What is it about Hetfield's guitar technique that makes him stand like a bare-chested colossus above all the other metal wannabees? Joel McIver's *The 100 Greatest Metal Guitarists* was a comprehensive assessment of all the great players within the genre and gave excellent insight into his significance: "Hetfield scraped away at the strings like some kind of single-minded robot, cupping his hand around the bridge for a perfectly taut sound that made heavy metal sound not brash nor rude nor sexy but more like the future. The apocalypse had arrived, and it came in the shape of the right hand of a spotty teenager from the wrong side of the LA tracks."

McIver perfectly captured Hetfield's guitar style. Hetfield told McIver how he approaches rhythm tempos: "I'm pretty comfortable with my down-picking. I don't see how it could get much faster. It's not a race. It's not really about ability: it's writing a good riff and knowing what tempo it needs to be, where it lives in the song."

The "down-picking" that Hetfield refers to is a technical guitar term, and for those not familiar, it's the downward stroke of the pick against the strings. Sometimes that downstroke is followed by an upstroke in the opposite direction, but in the case of some of Metallica's most effective riffs, the taut sound is a result of repeated downstrokes only.

It's worth mentioning that Hetfield's look while wielding a guitar is a contributing factor to his iconic status. While some guitarists look as if the instrument is a six-stringed alien appendage, Hetfield's always looks as if it's a permanent extension of his torso.

While his customary posture—with his left leg a full step in front of the right, his knees slightly bent and his body hunched menacingly over the microphone—was more effective in his days of long unruly hair, he still cuts a hugely iconic figure—one you too can try to emulate in your living room.

The guitar itself is part of the look, of course, and over the years, Hetfield has brandished a few weapons with which we can easily identify. There is the white ESP Explorer with "EET FUK" emblazoned on it, although this guitar now lies retired in the Rock & Roll Hall of Fame. That guitar suited him perfectly, and while numerous variations of that offset Explorer shape have been deployed in battle over the years, nothing looked quite as cool as this one did during the *Master of Puppets* era.

Of secondary consideration is his "Truckster," another ESP guitar, but this time in the more conservative shape of a Les Paul, which the manufacturer Gibson made famous as far back as the early 1950s. If you revisit *Some Kind of Monster*, you'll see Hetfield scratching out most of *St. Anger*'s sludgy riffs on a guitar much like this one.

Of equal significance is James's unusual vocal delivery, which is not even questioned nowadays because we have become accustomed to how he sounds. His vocals are not what classicists would call "singing" in the purest sense, particularly prior to 1991, but his style during the *Kill 'Em All* and *Ride the Lightning* eras perfectly suited a new kind of music.

"What I got out of time in the early days was that he wasn't a rock singer," suggested Anthrax's Charlie Benante, who has been a witness to James's progression as a singer since the early days. "It was all about aggression and angst. You wouldn't consider James a Freddie Mercury type, but it totally paved the way for what was to come."

Chuck Billy does not have the added distraction of playing a guitar while fronting Testament, although he makes up for that by replicating every note of every riff while clutching his microphone stand, as if he wished he did have a guitar. Billy is another peer who has a huge amount of respect for James's vocal presence: "To me he was probably one of the first power metal singers, or thrash metal guys, that actually came out and had hooks and melodies in the vocals. That's what I really liked about James. How catchy the choruses were and how clever the lyrics were. When you put the music that he was playing on top of all that, I was, like, 'Wow!' I always thought James was one of the best songwriters and lyricists to date."

Friend, who definitely has a way with words, took it one step further: "As a front man, he delivers each and every night the growl and groove that has made Metallica what they are. They reign supreme as one of the finest live bands in the history of rock 'n' roll because they leave nothing in the bag. It's a concert bonfire and James holds the brightest torch."

With such glowing testimony, you could say that Hetfield has worked hard on his vocal style over the years. Considering that for many years he didn't want to be a singer at all, the level he has achieved is a great credit to his perseverance.

There is one more person to thank for that: Bob Rock. Before "The Black Album" shook the rock world to its foundations in 1991, you would have been hard-pressed to find many harmonies from Hetfield. The band dabbled in textured vocals on tunes like "Fade to Black," but there was a feeling that it was half-hearted and that it wasn't done with any real confidence.

When Rock arrived on the scene as a producer, much of that changed. Because of his background with bands whose sound relied on harmony, Rock knew that if he could combine Metallica's muscle with a little vocal finesse, he had a match made in rock heaven.

The results, as we all know now, were absolutely stunning. While tracks like "Nothing Else Matters" and "The Unforgiven" were far removed from the ethos of a thrash metal band, those kinds of harmonies took Metallica to a new level of commercial acceptance. Remember his Brea Olinda High School prediction? *Play music, get rich* . . .

No assessment of Hetfield would be complete without acknowledging another part of his incredible armory. We know he's a great guitarist and an iconic singer and front man. We might even be persuaded that James is a likeable and often misunderstood person. However, to justify our imminent placement of James Hetfield among the true legends of popular music—the Dylans, the Springsteens, the Bonos and even the Madonnas—we have to consider his songwriting and lyrical ability.

Forget that Metallica operate in a genre far removed from all of the above. Songwriting is songwriting. The test is whether you can sustain it over time and in a way that propels your band from point A to point B, when others fall by the wayside. When Metallica came out of the underground, they did so on the back of not just tight riffs, aggressive singing and a confrontational attitude. They did it because of killer songs that seized the attention of an entire generation and dragged them screaming into the future.

Whether the so-called establishment likes it or not, heavy metal is a massively influential movement. When a band comes along that can not only reinvent a genre but also launch it headlong into the mainstream, their importance cannot be overstated.

While Lars Ulrich can take credit for some of this progress, his main strengths lie elsewhere. Consequently, in this author's opinion, James Hetfield is the man responsible for much of the songwriting genius that is Metallica—although obviously Ulrich and Hammett deserve huge credit also.

When we look at how a guy like Hetfield managed to construct such incredible songs, we need only refer to the testimony of that guy from his adolescence, Hugh Tanner. All those years ago in a bedroom in Brea, Tanner knew that the person he was jamming with had a knack for assembling kick-ass rock songs—and all that from just a collection of crudely assembled guitar riffs. Bands like Led Zeppelin did the same thing, of course, but they used a blues-based approach that made their task much easier. Hetfield did not have such a blueprint, but he did have disparate influences, from Aerosmith to The Tygers of Pan Tang, and what he came up with sounded like nothing we had ever heard.

While true fans of Metallica will always have a soft spot for the first four albums, the biggest stroke of genius came in the form of 1991's *Metallica*, where Hetfield, as Friend said, "used his musical genius to create the monster that is 'Black.'"

It's the kind of album that comes along only once or twice every half-century. That, combined with its thermonuclear sales success, is sufficient to ensure Hetfield's songwriting immortality. Part of the appeal of these incredible tracks is the lyrics, and Hetfield scratches them out in that now familiar spidery style, with a painstaking attention to detail that seizes the listener's attention.

His lyrics always have a point. They either paint a picture, describe a person or champion a cause. They are always compelling and sometimes bitter but, at the same time, witty and sarcastic. Hetfield the master songwriter is also a lyrical genius and every bit as worthy as a Dylan or a Springsteen in both respects.

But what of James Hetfield? What is his role in the now-evolved Metallica picture? In many ways, he is where he always has been: in control.

"James is a total fuckin' control freak; he's been in control all the time," Pantera's Rex Brown confirmed. "Lars is the spokesperson, but what James says kind of fuckin' goes. You've seen the movie, man. Those guys could have got up and left and said 'Well, fuck you!' you know. He was going through a fuckin' tough time, he had problems at that time, they *all* had problems at that time."

Brown believes things are different now: "It's easy to get caught up in thinking that you are some kind of god. James isn't like that now and he's brought some of that into the team of Metallica. He realizes that he can't always do it all on his own."

While James's personal battles have undeniably thrown a few obstacles onto his path over the years, his place in the overall fabric of music is more important than ever. Malcolm Dome, who has observed Hetfield's phenomenal rise to prominence from a critical standpoint over the last twenty-five years, agreed: "I think James is a vitally important figure in music, and I think that importance has become more over the last ten or so years."

The last dozen or so years, the most public period of Hetfield's career, have coincided with a radical change in the way that the media, and the world in general, view people, particularly famous people. Katon De Pena, an old friend of Hetfield's from LA, still keeps in touch via mutual friends like Brian Slagel. He felt strongly about the personal side of the matter: "James is a great guy. Sometimes I feel that he is misunderstood. I think some people should keep in mind that if you don't really know him . . . you don't have the right to judge him."

ACKNOWLEDGEMENTS

Before the Internet and cell phones, info about awesome bands playing in the Bay Area and memorable shows was often relayed back to Los Angeles and other areas via letters between friends with similar interests. Some of these buddies are here in this book as a result—a few of them discussing events for the first time—and it's been an honor to exist in their world for even a short part of my life.

It was a conversation with Joel McIver back in 2005 that marked the beginning of this journey. I had just read his excellent *Justice for All: The Truth About Metallica*. (If you haven't read it, you need to immediately—*after* you've finished this, of course.) He made the mistake of including his e-mail address . . .

Sporadic communication followed over the next couple of years, mostly about Metallica and more regularly nowadays about more normal matters. Without Joel I would not be writing this book and I'll always be grateful to him.

As for the others who have helped, here is a list in no particular order, and they're *all* important: Martin Roach and Dave Hanley at

Independent Music Press, Ron Quintana, Brian Slagel, Bill Hale, Brian Lew, Ron McGovney, Mike Tacci, Eric Braverman, Fred Cotton, David Ellefson, Charlie Benante (Anthrax), Bob Nalbandian (Hardradio), Jerry Cantrell (Alice in Chains), Brian Fair (Shadows Fall), Malcolm Dome (Total Rock Radio), David Tedder, Katon De Pena (Hirax), Alex Skolnick (Testament, Trans Siberian Orchestra and The Alex Skolnick Band), Chuck Billy (Testament), Dave Marrs, Hugh Tanner, John Kornarens, Michael Alago, Flemming Rasmussen, Lloyd Grant, Mille Petrozza (Kreator), Lonn Friend, Bobby Schneider, Dan Beehler (Exciter, Beehler), Jeff Waters (Annihilator), Michael Wagener, Sammy DeJohn, Jim Durkin (Dark Angel), Rex Brown (Pantera, Down), Rikki Zazula (Adrenaline PR), James Arnold and Jonny Zazula.

ABOUT THE AUTHOR

Mark Eglinton is the cowriter of *Official Truth, 101 Proof: The Inside Story of Pantera* by Rex Brown of Pantera and *Confessions of a Heretic: The Sacred and the Profane: Behemoth and Beyond* by Adam Nergal Darski of Behemoth. He lives in Carlsbad, California.

For more information, go to www.mark-eglinton.com.